As Fathers Go

by

Anandavalli Nair

For Achan
And the other Raghavan

1

Thalassery -- A verdant, little, coastal town, tucked away in the South-Western corner of India along the shores of the Arabian Sea. If you walk a long, long way north hugging the coast you will finally reach Mumbai (formerly Bombay.) If instead, you walk in the opposite direction, you will end up in the Indian Ocean, quite quickly, somewhere near Sri Lanka. I always thought that Kerala, our state, was where the rain was born.

When I travelled from Chennai to Thalassery by the old Madras Mail Train, I would see how the terrain changed from barren brown to rich green as we came out of the tunnel, through the Western Ghats. I'd press my eager head into the horizontal bars of the train-window and breathe deep of that familiar smell of wet vegetation and home. With it I would also take in the particles of soot and ash that came out of the front of the steam engine, making my eyes itch and my hair gritty.

Well before the fears of global warming and consequent flooding, the monsoons arrived with predictable regularity each year, at the end of June, and swept away a few houses nestling precariously on the top of river-bunds.

There was no welfare state, so the community, neighbours, had to step in. After several days of unrelenting downpour, the waters would rise and spread.

My father's sister would have spent the whole month of *Karkadagam*, (the Malayalam month that falls between the middle of July and the middle of August known for disease, death and devastation) chanting prayers to ward off the disasters. During this period, the streak of *bhasmam* (sacred ash) on her forehead got a little longer and thicker, just in case her devotion was in any way suspect.

Generally smallpox, chickenpox, typhoid and plague, arrived in the rainy season. The old women in the house, whose duty it was to guard against all evils that could be fended off with prayer and incantation read out of the holy book, *Bhagavatham*, at dusk and dawn, in front of the *nilavilakku*, the sacred lamp. But, of course, chickenpox ignored the holy chants and spread through the house and went. No one was too concerned as chicken pox didn't usually kill. It lingered with one person or another and all of us in the house waited for it to strike. It was a community illness in that it generally spread through a whole neighbourhood before moving on.

Our extended household had three children: myself and my father's brother's children, Mani and Appu, Mani six months older and Appu four years older. My father's niece, Naani, father's sister whom I called *Ammamma* and father's mother, Achamma (paternal grandmother), also lived there. So chicken pox had quite a haul.

Achamma always organised her second line of defence when disease got close – as in next door.

She kept coconut shells filled with a cow-dung solution along both sides of our walkway to the front gate; this was supposed to ward off *Mariamma*, the evil goddess of smallpox. Maybe the same Goddess did duty for chickenpox too. I had a mental image of this vile witch, grotesque and pock-marked. She haunted my dreams; she was always hanging about our front gate, working her way up to the house.

Early in the morning every day, I would see Achamma, bent like a question mark, making her way slowly down the walkway to the gate, checking the coconut shells. Her hair, in old age, had become scant and short, just shoulder-length, and it was nearly blonde; it looked golden when it caught the sun, and sometimes I would tease her calling her *Madamma* (white woman) because of the colour of her hair.

Achamma had very little energy – she was close to seventy-five years old at a time when people in India celebrated *shashtipoorthy*, the birthday when you reached sixty years. Indians, in those days had no durability beyond forty years; thirty-five was middle-aged, fifty was old. So whatever she was doing would consume all her energy and she would not see anything else. She didn't take any notice of me anyway; she was totally devoid of humour. Also, she had no time for girls, only boys counted.

In any case, Achamma had lost her eldest son to smallpox when he was twenty-one years old, so she couldn't be reassured. She inspected the chickenpox rash on Naani's forehead daily and declared some of them were in fact smallpox pustules.

Smallpox actually kept its distance from the house because we had all been vaccinated, with those long-handled pen-shaped needles, the prick of which was pure agony. The end was shaped like a sharp circular screw, and it had to be turned through an excruciating three-hundred-and sixty degrees as the vaccine was released. It would leave an angry, round wound in the upper arm where it was administered, which hopefully would suppurate and declare the vaccination effective. And we, children, would examine the mark daily, praying for it to get inflamed; if it didn't we would have to be vaccinated again. Achamma had no faith in any of that and refused to be vaccinated.

Smallpox died out in India gradually as the vaccinations reached the villages and all the schools. In my generation, no one died of smallpox. My uncle and a few women in our family had pitted faces from smallpox; the deaths were random – some in any household survived with scarred faces, others died. Of my father's two brothers, the eldest had died some years ago, and the younger survived with a pock-marked face.

In the period, 1941 to 1947, I got measles twice. Measles was taken lightly, probably because it didn't kill as many people as the other diseases did. If you lost an eye, it was probably because you had neglected the strict diet prescribed by the local medicine man. The second time a rash appeared on me, Ammamma (father's sister) kept saying it could not be measles, measles never strikes the same person twice.

The *vaidyan* (the local medicine man), came to look at my measles-like rash and confirmed measles; he prescribed a herbal remedy called a *Kashayam*. He wrote a long list of herbs and roots, which would

4

be boiled in water and left overnight to steep in a clay pot. I had to drink it three times a day. Getting it down was quite a feat; it tasted like boiled, pulped tree, mixed with clay. Ammamma would give me a block of *vellam* (unrefined brown sugar) to help it to go down.

And then there was *pathyam* – a rigorous protocol of 'don't eats.' Anything cooked in oil was taboo; indeed the household was discouraged from cooking any food in fat because it would slow the cure and help the disease to spread to others.

During 1942, there were rumours of cholera in town; there did not appear to be any treatment for it. Cholera killed large numbers, mainly from the poorest parts of Thalassery. Nobody boiled drinking water in those days; our own water came from the well in our house, which was home to several frogs. Occasionally a rat might die in there, and we had to sterilise the water with crystals of Potassium Permanganate. Our water would be light pink water for a few days, and after three days the well would be declared harmless.

When I went to Sierra Leone on behalf of the British Council, in 1983, the initial briefing document insisted I had to boil every drop of water I drank, and all vegetables, including salad leaves, had to be cooked. Needless to say I found all this a bit extreme. (But then, they also asked me to attend a weekend of pre-post briefing in a holiday home in Kent, to learn about how to live in the tropics. A woman who had spent some years working in Africa would be there to induct us. I had half a mind to go for the break and a laugh, if nothing else, but my conscience was stern, so I didn't.)

I boiled the water as I had been instructed, but definitely did not cook my salads. Today, I drink water out of the taps in England, but many of my friends remind me about lead in the old pipes. When the quotidian life gets too complicated, my instinct is to simplify. I am a disciple of Thoreau, who taught me to *'Simplify, Simplify.'*

As I was growing up in Thalassery, in the forties, it seemed to me that every household lived with various illnesses; children were falling ill frequently and whether they would live or not appears to have been a matter of luck. When a child is born in Kerala, the time and day are noted down by the astrologer in what is known as a *charthu,* a parchment. A horoscope is then developed from this initial note after five years, the assumption being that a child's existence until then is so precarious, fate should not be tempted.

In the house to the right of ours, there were many children and there was always illness of one kind or another. In one year, when I was eight years old, a child in that house coughed for long spells in the night, when the neighbourhood was asleep. I knew that boy because his older sister was my age and I occasionally played with her. We could hear him clearly in the night when the little traffic in that small town ceased. It was an agonising cough that went on for hours keeping me up in the small hours of the night; it would stop for a minute sometimes, making me believe the little boy was now over that coughing fit; then it would start again. That whooping cough lingered in our neighbour's house for many months going from one child to another.

Appu, my cousin, contracted typhoid, when he

was eleven years old. He was ill for three weeks, recovered, and had a relapse. Appu was prescribed a diet of loose-jacket oranges and pears when he started recovering and this was good news for me. We girls, Mani and I, were meant to keep our distance and respect the quarantine, but the fruit was there to take. Appu handed it to us through the wooden window slats.

When Appu had his relapse and became rake thin, Achan (father) took to going into the sick-room straight from the Courts after work, dumping his gown on the floor outside. One day, when Appu's fever was high, Achan cried, which was the most frightening thing of all, and Appu cried with him. There were no antibiotics then. Appu, recovered after a long two months and the rest of us escaped.

When he recovered, Appu was a shadow of himself. A wraith-like boy with his prominent front teeth now even more prominent on his skeletal face. For many months after, Appu had to drink tonics to return him to the sprightly, naughty boy that he had been.

The scourge of those times, however, was Bubonic Plague. It was rare. Across from us was a large, half-finished house set in a big garden, with a pond next to it. The man who started building that ambitious house had gone to Malaysia just before the beginning of the Second World War in the Far East and didn't return till the fifties. In his absence, vagrants took the place over and used it for all the chicaneries usually indulged in by young men looking for easy excitement with not much money. During the period when the owner was languishing in Singapore, someone had hung himself from the rafters of the porch, so locals, other than the young gangs, gave the place a wide berth, saying the ghost of the man who committed suicide haunted the house.

Plague, when it came, lingered in that shell of a house for many months. A family of migrants lived there when the vagrants abdicated for other pastures; they lived in the porch, cooked on three-stone fires and washed in the pond in the compound. There were two men in the family, who looked like brothers, two young women and many children, all under the age of ten. Often the women came to our house, making signs asking for old clothes, sometimes food. Clearly, they were Indian, but they didn't speak our language and we couldn't guess where they had come from.

Mani and I were strictly forbidden from going to the house because of the pond, but we couldn't resist; we would sneak off when no one was watching and stare at the group. The women would smile and call out to us, but the language frustrated us, so we just hung about. However, when the family started dying the women would chase us away.

Plague killed off the family one by one. There was no money for funerals and no place to bury the dead, so the municipal shit cart would come and carry the bodies away; Mani and I watched through our windows and cried.

Those children never had any kind of life. They didn't look that different from us, except that their faces and clothes were dirty and they didn't seem to go to school. When the family had been reduced to just the father and a young girl they abandoned their broken clay pots and their infected clothes and just walked away. One morning they were not there. A few days later, a man from the Municipality came around to spray Phenyl on the premises. The cart had T.M.C in large letters on its side – Thalassery Municipal Council. We called it *theetam, moothram, kashtam* -- shit, piss and rubbish.

In those pre-independence days most of the treatment for *any* disease, consisted of herbal medicines. There was a herbal medicine vendor about a mile from our house, and as I travelled daily to school in my rickshaw I would see him chopping leaves and roots and other vegetation on a two-foot tree trunk he used as a chopping board. The medicines were vile tasting.

The *Vaidyan* (indigenous doctor) was always the first port of call for illness in the family. Unless my father got involved, which he rarely did, because no one told him about stomach pains or back pains. Doctors trained in Western medicine were rarities in Thalassery in the thirties and forties. We had one – Kunhikkannan doctor. My father went to him, and he took me too for childhood ailments. For most things, I remember,

Ammamma would go down to the compound and pick what looked like weeds to me. But she knew which herb did what. She brewed them for many hours and strained them; they worked. This is a knowledge that has now been lost; after Ammamma, no one in our family knew anything about those herbs.

Ammamma prescribed a laxative for most illnesses: Senna pods stewed and strained. Mani and I did not mention small aches and pains to her for fear of that concoction. The alternative was cod liver oil – not much to choose from.

We had one dentist; when my milk teeth started coming loose, my father would take me to the dentist, to take the tooth out gently with a steel instrument. If that didn't happen, Ammamma would tie a knot with thread round the tooth where it met the gum; the other end would be tied to an open door. She would then slam the door suddenly and the tooth would come off. She didn't give me a sweet after the extraction like the dentist. It was a question of who got there first – Achan or Ammamma

By the fifties we had two or three trained doctors, all men, and in the late fifties, we had our first lady doctor. During that period, gradually, the faith in western medicine grew and the *vaidyans* lost ground.

Recently clinics have sprung up all over Kerala, offering Ayurvedic treatment or Homeopathic treatment. Medical schools in India offer these options as specialisms in the third and fourth years of a medical degree, and the take-up is enthusiastic. When I am in India, I often spend a week at an Ayurvedic Nursing home. It is a kind of pampering unavailable with the NHS. The oil massages are deeply soporific during and after the massage. The food is vegetarian and oil-free; I find I lose half a stone of weight in one week. Meditation events are included, and if you are determined, you can keep up the discipline and continue to enjoy the benefits after returning home.

My Homeopathy doctor knows more about my body and mind than I do, and a great deal more than the fragmented me that the NHS sees; his initial diagnostic meeting is always over an hour long. The treatment is delivered through tiny pills as they are in England. Those pills have never once let me down: they have no side effects, no stomach angst.

It took only ten days for the doctor to cure me of three food allergies, that had plagued me for decades, and the same amount of time to get rid of rashes picked up in the garden, talking to my irritable Dieffenbachia, or from insect bites indoors. My children, who have lived here in England from early childhood, do not trust either treatment. They are amused that I go to these 'quacks.' They think it is my Indian origins that give me faith in this kind of 'superstition.' The arrogance! I go by proven efficacy of both Homeopathic and Ayurvedic treatments.

Having experienced the disasters that the monsoon brings, I am wary of the monsoon season even now, in my old age; I remember it as the time when most of the deadly diseases like cholera and plague attacked our community. Now, even though the scourges of those years have been conquered, I still avoid going to India during those monsoon months. Today there are new diseases to avoid: Dengue fever and in some parts of India, Malaria. When I was a young child in Thalassery, we didn't need mosquito nets – indeed we didn't have one in the house. Now, even in the villages, where houses and people are not living in close and unhealthy proximity, mosquitoes will not let you sleep without fans or nets.

The annual arrival of the Southwest Monsoon was exciting to all – students, for possible days off from school, farmers for the promise of healthy rice crops,

11

all households for relief from the summer heat...
Just as I did, my father liked following the course of
floods. When it had rained steadily for several days,
my father would sit on the very edge of the veranda,
watching the water level rise. He saw it as a contest
between man and nature and waited to see who
would win. Visitors would discuss the rains
endlessly as the weather is discussed in England. The
kitchen would be littered with pots and pans of all
shapes to catch the roof-leaks and a thin coir rope
would be strung across the stone fireplace, to dry our
uniforms. The whole house would smell of mould.

When it became clear that the rising floods had
won, my father's compassion and sense of
community would kick in. He would spring into
action, insisting that I gathered up my spare clothes
to offer to families, who had lost all that they owned.
I was quite selfish and didn't want to part with
anything to donate to the people washed up like
flotsam on the banks of neighbourhood rivers. I
didn't have many items of spare clothes, so my
father's instructions caused a great deal of heart-
searching. Was there anything I had outgrown, or
torn beyond rescue? On one occasion, when I did not
cooperate quickly enough, he went to the rope in the
compound, where the day's wash was drying, and
pulled out a skirt and blouse from it. I lost my
favourite skirt and learned my lesson. When I
complained, Achan said, 'You'll survive.'

Schools always re-opened early in June, after the
fierce, humid heat of the summer months. Rains
came generally in the last week of June, petering out
after a fair share of death and destruction had been

achieved, sometime in early August. On the first day of the monsoon, just before the skies opened, the frogs would announce the arrival of the sight-and-sound show. The birds would fly hurriedly to their nests as the sky darkened. The thunder, (my father said it was the Gods moving furniture in the heavens) would drive the frightened snakes deep into their holes in the ground, but when the rains stopped, the petrichor would bring them out again, to slither joyfully in the mud. That smell of new rain-washed mud must be one of the delights of a tropical inheritance. Now it has been obliterated by petrol and diesel fumes; one has to travel deep into the villages to experience that heady smell again.

Rainy mornings in Thalassery had a soporific quality – In my childhood I would sit on the floor of my veranda and watch the water-level rise in our yard, daring it to touch the cement floor; it never did. I would do it for hours, with my thumb stuck into some hole in my petticoat, which could, with a little imagination, pass for a frock. I lived in those two-piece slips, all white, put together quite casually by our tailor, who plied his uncertain trade in a corner of the little shop left of our gate. When my father realised I spent most of my hours at home in those slips, he got the tailor to make me four coloured ones, which I loved. Untold riches!

Those days, sticking my thumb into a tear in my garment was my childhood equivalent of sucking my thumb – or meditation. The cement on the veranda steps was cold and rough. My bum generally suffered, but the heavy raindrops falling on the puddles under the eaves made a rare and pretty picture. Where the sun caught the bubbles in the morning, light slanting through moving coconut fronds, split into rainbow hues. I was child enough at six and seven years to believe that I could catch that colour; I would stretch my palm out and the rainbow would settle on my hands. Magic! Quite often I would be drenched as the winds drove the sheets of water in many directions.

We lived near the railway lines later; indeed, we could see the trains chugging along, on the other side of the *Koduvally* river, with their head of steam, from our veranda. I thought of that railway line as mine because my beloved maternal grandfather worked as a Guard on the South India Railway.

On the road to the railway lines, which was one of my father's favourite morning walks, he would often point out the huts of the poor, lean-tos put together with coconut fronds, sheets of corrugated iron, cardboard and tarpaulin. They were never more than three metres long, and narrow, to fit on the width of the raised banks of the Koduvally river. Children, half-naked, played on the soggy surroundings of their homes and when we walked by, almost another species with our dry clothes and our certainties, they stared at us as at another life-form. Everything -- their clothes, their faces, their bodies, their huts – all seemed to be the uniform dispiriting colour of clay.

Indeed, the river was lined with houses on one side, and the railway line on the other. The latrines of the houses flanking the river were built precariously over the edge of the compounds, partly over the river, on coconut trunks driven into the water. I once asked my father what would happen if the folks in those houses fell into the river while defecating. 'Then they wouldn't need to wash after,'

14

he answered with scant mercy.

2

The years of my childhood were also the years of famine in parts of India, especially Bengal, and extreme poverty in many states. One of the regular sights of Thalassery in the forties was the steady procession of beggars; an unending, sad stream of them in the streets and in the doorways. They came to the richer houses in Thalassery every day, and soon learned to differentiate between the kind and the cold-blooded. They made the universal sign of begging for food -- touching their mouths and opening their palms. I remember the terrible procession of shabby, hungry and hopeless families.

In our house, Achamma saved dry coconut shells for the beggars to drink *conjee* out of, and when our rice was drained daily, she set aside a few handfuls, that she would drop into the starchy water drained from the rice. She would keep this in a clay-pot; around three in the afternoon, the clay pot would be empty and she would have to turn away the remaining procession of beggars. Gradually, the beggars learned to clock in before that three o'clock 'closing' time.

I would look at the children of around my age or younger, clinging to their mothers' garments or hiding behind them. My family would not let me go within touching distance of them; Ammamma warned that they might be carrying infectious diseases. I wondered, where were the fathers, rarely to be seen with them? Where were the older children?

When it had rained continuously for many days and the water-levels rose enough to create mayhem and destruction, my father and I would walk to our little beach, only five minutes from where we lived, to see the objects the sea had claimed.

Unlike famine, which may have been avoided, the rain wreaked economic havoc of a different sort locally. Whole barns, full of *copra*, (coconuts dried for months to be milled and made into coconut oil, were generally stored in barns made from bamboo poles tied with coir rope.) would lift off from the banks of rivers, where they were situated, and float into the sea; you could see them bobbing away gracefully towards the horizon. Someone's livelihood for the next year washed away. The sea would be an ominous gun-metal grey, and occasionally, far away, there would be a huge shark tossing and turning with the water.

So, for me, rain-washed Thalassery is where it all began.

In 1933, my mother, Janaki, all of fourteen years old, got engaged to my quicksilver father, Raghavan. Quicksilver, because of his sudden changing moods and incessant pursuit of goals he set himself – reading, swimming in the sea, gardening, walking...

A*chan* (father) was somewhat older than my amma (mother) and better educated, naturally. She barely reached standard nine before she was offered to my father's family. What did education have to do with females? Achan started in the local Government Brennen College, which provided for only two years of post-school education after matriculation, then called school-finals. F A, the qualification was called, Fellow of Arts; about the standard of British A levels.

To most men in that small town, Thalassery, finals would have meant just that. Time to stop all that school nonsense and start earning a living. The women, in those days didn't get that far. The Nairs lived off their lands and didn't aspire to do much with their lives. Malayalam enjoys a phonetic alphabet, which meant once you learned to read and write the fifty-four squiggles, you were literate by definition. Men and women attended the first two or three years in local one-room primary schools and became 'literate.' All the women in our family, of my father's generation, could read and write, but 'educated' they were not.

My father and a few others also attended these thatched, one-room village schools where one teacher taught all the children, cane in hand. The only difference with my father and two of his friends from the same village was that they decided to walk the four miles to town to attend the next level of education, and then the next. These three were the first three young men from his village, Kodiyeri, who graduated. (In my father's family, I was the first woman who went to college.) Achan would therefore have been considered a good catch in the marriage market. There were a few hiccups – he was the kind of man who would instigate hiccups whatever he did and wherever he went.

18

At the time, early twentieth century, most of the lecturers in Brennen College, Thalassery, were British, mainly Scottish. The story goes that my father took umbrage at an imagined insult, made by the lecturer, which involved the phrase, *'your father.'* I gathered my father was late to the lecture. The lecturer, from another culture, would have had no way of knowing that you simply did not use that phrase *'your father'* contemptuously, as part of an admonition, anywhere in Kerala. When my father tried to explain why he was late, the lecturer retorted, 'I am not interested in your father or your grandfather.' My father apparently staged a walk-out, and being who he was, it would have been a dramatic exit. Whereupon two of his friends also walked out behind him, in support. They had started an incident, which would lead to life-changing events in all three lives. Indeed, one of them never went back to his studies.

All three, to begin with, were suspended from the college. They could be reinstated if they offered a public apology. Two of them refused, the other apologised and returned to his studies. Later, my father admitted to me in passing, that in that atmosphere of nascent and aggressive nationalism, the young men were looking out for anything they could represent as a grievance.

The institution was a government college and no other college in the State of Madras would offer my father a place to continue his studies. (This Brennen College was established by Edward Brennen, an Englishman, who worked in Thalassery Port and made his home in Thalassery in the late nineteenth century.) It took my father a long time to be accepted by any college, and in the end, it was a private institution in far off Madanapalle, in Andhra State, which offered him sanctuary, and hope.

The Theosophical College in Madanapalle was established in the name of Annie Besant. (Annie Besant, an Irish woman, devoted her life, fruitlessly as it turned out, to the idea of a caste-less Indian society. She helped establish the Benares Hindu University and worked tirelessly to promote Indian culture. She was also the president of the Congress Party in India in 1917.) Here, my father completed his degree in History. He told me it was a harsh life; he had to go to college, far from home, in a place where he had to rent accommodation, and pay for train-travel to and from his home. He went home only for the summer holidays, once a year.

He settled into a corner of the veranda of a local house for a small rent. They let him cook his daily rice and dhal in that corner, and he bathed by diving into the well in the compound. Apparently, he would put his rice and dhal in one pot, which was all the kitchen utensils he possessed, and go off for a bath while the food cooked. He told me a story of how, once, he got winded in his dive and couldn't surface for a while. His food was burnt to cinder by the time he managed to come up and get to his pot.

Achan had to fight for his education. There is a story in the family that he went on hunger-strike for a week to persuade his impecunious parent to fund his law degree. Apparently, *Achachan* (paternal grandfather) had to sell his ancestral home to finance my father's ambitions. Apocryphal or not, I could imagine this relentless pursuit of his goal; he was a stubborn man.

20

After he graduated, he did a law degree in Madras (now Chennai in Tamil Nadu). There was also professional training in Thiruvananthapuram, in Kerala, for a year, before he could practise law in his hometown. He was then twenty-six years old. Malayalam was his mother-tongue, as is mine, but in Madras and Madanappalle he learned a smattering of Tamil and Telungu and became fluent in the English language, representing his college at many debates and winning silver medals and other accolades.

When I was about sixteen years old I came across a horde of medals in a tin box in his chest of drawers; Achan said I could pick one and put it on a chain if I wished. I got the local goldsmith to attach it to my necklace and displayed this heart-shaped medal proudly on my person.

'Why do you spoil your nice gold chain with this cheap pendant?' my friends asked. I described with pride how I came by that silver locket; I still have it in my jewel box.

The languages my father acquired in Madras and Madanapalle would stand him in good stead when he was in prison in Vellore, and later Tanjore, in the war years. The freedom fighters immured in those prisons were from all over India and he had to become polyglot in a hurry. It was British policy to send the men as far away from their homes as possible, preferably to another state – this would prevent them from fraternising with the warders and other prisoners. None of this worked of course. When the Andaman Islands were occupied by the Japanese, the prisoners were informed by the warders; the warders sneaked newspapers into the wards when something momentous happened, so the inmates knew all about the course of the freedom struggle, as well as the armed struggle going on in the Far East and in Europe at that time.

3

In those days, that is in the early twentieth century, in the Nair caste to which both my parents belonged, engagement was an event organised by the elders, and because it was a matrilineal society, with inheritance passing down the female line, from uncle to niece, rather than father to children, this engagement was masterminded by my mother's uncle. It might have been mentioned in passing to the child-bride-to-be by her mother, if she was lucky. The uncles, in those days, took responsibility for feeding and clothing their nieces and nephews, finding husbands and wives when the time came, and conducting the weddings.

The *kaniyan*, the local astrologer, was the central figure in this event; he would decide whether the horoscopes of the prospective partners matched; he would even pronounce on their sexual compatibility (*yoni porutham*), without seeing either of them. He generally came with a bagful of cowrie shells and a piece of chalk. A representative from the prospective bridegroom's family would attend to approve the decisions. I remember the sense of occasion connected to the arrival of the *kaniyan* in any house. Generally, there were only a handful of them catering to the community, and everyone knew them by sight. They came at moments of significance in a household, heralding weddings, naming ceremonies, funerals... The *kaniyan*, it was, who would decide what were auspicious times and dates for starting journeys to foreign countries, or even when to have a housewarming.

There would be the sacred *nilavilakku* (lamp) presiding over the ceremony. Of course. The *kaniyan* would draw some columns and lines on the floor, a complicated noughts-and-crosses shape in front of the ceremonial lamp. Then he would start arranging the shells within his diagram, according to the horoscopes of the prospective bride and bridegroom.

After placing the shells he would 'read' them. He would chant Sanskrit verses, justifying every prediction made by him. The men of the house would sit around him, leaning forward, listening avidly, even if they did not understand a word of Sanskrit. Women would hover near the windows in the corridors behind to get a whiff of the decision being formed.

If the horoscopes of the bride and the groom 'matched,' especially the positions of Saturn, Mars and the Sun in the firmament when they were born, he would ceremoniously tie the two horoscopes together. (I should know, because Saturn was in all the wrong places in my horoscope, and so I was able to escape marriage for a very long time.) After that the *kaniyan* would suggest auspicious dates for the wedding and leave with his fee, a few coins, tucked into the waist of his *mundu* (white dothi).

The marriage ceremony itself was a non-event. The point of it was to permit a man and a woman to sleep together and produce off-spring. The ritual was minimal. A garlanding of the bride and groom, with jasmine garlands if they were available, in front of the lighted *nilavilakku*, in the *padingitta*, the puja room of the house. A few family members and neighbours would be watching. Then a feast, which would go on till late in the night because Nair weddings took place at night. Somewhere, in between, the bride would be led to the nuptial bed and the door of the chamber closed firmly behind her, by one of her paternal aunts. *There you are then, go forth and copulate.*

I wait hopefully, for the time when Indians can live together a while and test the waters out before they get married to partners of their own choice. Even in the villages. I would happily endorse a few dirty weekends here and there. Definitely preferable to the head-long somersault into marriage.

And the sad part is, even to this day, marriages are hard to get out of. People look at the urban, educated professionals of India; obviously they find it easy to terminate marriages. They make their own choices; people looking in from the outside assume this is true of all of India. In villages, (and remember, ninety percent of India's population live in villages,) marriages are life-long, and women have to stay in them, however abusive or love-less they are.

For the man, it was always a matter of choice, and they did exercise that choice. As late as the end of the nineteenth century, men taking second and third wives was common. My aunt was a second wife, my great aunt was a first wife who had to suffer the humiliation of a second wife, in the same house, ensconced just down the corridor.

Here, again, there is an imbalance of power between a man and his wife. Add to that the fact that, in a joint family home, loyalties were fragmented, and the wife was dependent on the mercy of many people. She would have no financial resources of her own and no home of her own. Her own family would not countenance her return home with equanimity – they would try to send her back. Today's working women do not depend on husbands for income, do not meekly stay with their in-laws and are quite capable of going it alone.

When I left my husband in 1972, I didn't go back to India again for six years. After I'd experienced the slander and the harassment when I went home briefly, it took me a long time to summon up the courage to return. I was not invited to any family events during this period as I *'would bring misfortune on the event'* with my presence. I was *persona non-grata*.

I noticed that later, when I became financially independent I was accepted back -- for the same reason that professional women manage to get control of their lives. The common denominator in all these situations is money. And shelter. For a woman, in my book, the most important safeguards are a place to live and an income. The home doesn't have to be owned, rented would be fine if you can afford the rent. If you don't have a place for you and your children to live, you are man-fodder.

With respect to the actual rituals accompanying weddings, things have changed in India in recent times. In Thalassery, which has managed to stay unscathed, pristine and undeveloped, even when the rest of Kerala is rapidly advancing within the twenty-first century, marriage ceremonies are no longer short or simple; diversity has entered in a big

27

way. Now, in 2017, the accretions over the decades to what was a simple, pared-down marriage-ritual confound me.

First there was the *thali*, the sacred chain round the neck, to be blessed by the pujari (holy man conducting the ceremony) and tied round the bride's neck by the groom. (No such leashes for him.) This would be removed only when she was widowed or dead, so it was a life-long encumbrance when bathing, swimming etc. I got rid of mine somewhere along the way when no one was looking, but I kept it in a quick-access place. In case. My husband was not interested enough to notice that my thali had gone. Or indeed that anything else about me had gone.

The thali was a distinctly South Malabar practice; my husband's family was from Palakkad, in South Malabar, though he grew up in Sri Lanka. I was from the North. Once upon a time, Nairs from the North and south of Malabar did not intermarry. South Malabar by our reckoning started some sixty-five miles south of Thalassery, the other side of the *Baratha puzha*, the notional boundary river, but things were changing fast.

Then the practice of exchanging rings arrived. In the past, it had been a Christian practice, but by 1957, families from Malabar were incorporating rings into the ceremony. Again, I took mine off at some unknown guest house while on the road and forgot it. My husband similarly got rid of his. Neither of us knew or cared where the rings had gone.

And in today's elaborate weddings, the close family and friends have to feed the bride and groom banana and milk after the wedding. So, the couple sit on a raised platform and suffer this procession of people thrusting spoons into their mouths. Where did *that* abomination come from?

Now, in the twenty-first century, the marriage rituals from all over India have coalesced somewhat in terms of their elasticity. Weddings can be anything from two to five days long, depending on the wealth of the bride's family and their inclination to show off. In one wedding in Paris a few years ago, a wealthy Indian patriarch flew in his guests from all over the world to attend his daughter's wedding. Even the *Mehndi* ceremony, now so popular in Kerala, came from the north of India; a whole day is devoted to it, drawing designs on the palms of the bride, and a cohort of invited girls.

A recent aberration, if you are really, disgustingly wealthy, is for family and guests to travel to a resort overseas like the Maldives or Sri-Lanka for the wedding, the father of the bride picking up the bill. Jesus wept!

I live in hope. Somewhere along the line, it might dawn on a little girl watching that the emperor's clothes are a matter of illusion.

Nair marriages were called *pudamuris*, (*pudava* -- cloth, and *muri* -- cutting), the cutting of cloth. The central part of the ceremony was the new roll of white cloth the bridegroom would bring with him. The *pujari (the holy man conducting the ceremony)* would cut it into two pieces at the *Muhurtham*, the auspicious time. The bridegroom would give one half to the bride and the other half to the aunt who had led her to the ceremony. This meant that he was now taking responsibility for providing the bride with clothes.

All that 'gelf' money that is flooding into Kerala and churning up the culture, the same Gulf-Dirhams, which are paying for the proliferation of concrete-roofed house in the villages of India, also encourage the elaborate weddings, which have now become common in Kerala.

The inflow of hard currency from the Gulf has paid for mosques, which vie for height with every other building in sight. In Moozhikkara, my father's village, the homes carefully arrange themselves a few feet below the local places of worship to keep the Gods appeased. They also preserve the landscape in harmony.

The mosques of my childhood were subdued and dignified; today they are all glitter and gaudiness. *Now*, if that money had been diverted to education, specifically to the education of Muslim women, who have some catching-up to do…I have spent my life in education and it has reinforced my belief that the only way to help different cultures and religions to live together in peace and goodwill is to educate the young in the same schools.

It must be admitted that when Christianity invaded India and the missionaries started proselytising, the first thing they did was establish schools near the churches and chapels. The alphabet and numbers went hand in hand with the Trinity. They also started small clinics and treated the illnesses they could manage, like Malaria and common coughs. However, the Catholics and Protestants exported their internecine squabbles overseas, where the two communities fought for turf.

The animosity between the Irish Catholics and

Protestants can only be finally put to rest when children of the two religions are educated in the same schools. This applies in England too – Tony Blair did no favours to anyone by establishing faith schools. If Muslims, Hindus, Christians, Jews etc. are to live together in peace, the children have to be thrown together into the same milieu when growing up.

It used to frustrate me when I went to Thalassery in the sixties that Muslim education was so far behind the rest of everyone else. Throughout my Primary and Secondary education, I came across two Muslim girls and one Muslim boy in my school. They never went beyond standard 4.

When I went to college, from 1950-1954, there was not a single Muslim girl, and in an institution of approximately eight-hundred students, there were just two Muslim men. Amazingly, we did have a delightful Muslim lecturer who taught History. In those days Muslims were mostly petty traders; a few businessmen became rich, but they did not send their children into education. Now, of course, Muslims in Kerala, have caught up with all others in education and careers.

When the first Muslim girl got to college, many years later, my father was elated. He wrote to me saying she had to be flanked by two policemen for the first few weeks when she walked to college, because there had been threats against her life from the fundamentalists. But she did it. He lived to see the Muslims, girls and boys, go to College as a matter of course, and into careers just like anyone else. He lived to see a Muslim man, a college-mate of mine, become the Chairman of the Public Service

Commission in Kerala. Where education is concerned Kerala doesn't give an inch; she just pushes and throws herself against the barricades in her way; she generally wins.

Initially Malabar, within which Thalassery snuggled, had been part of the Madras State as it was originally called, under British colonial rule. Kochi and Thiruvananthapuram had their Maharajas and operated independently of the central government. It is an interesting fact that one of the first places in Kerala to introduce free primary schooling was Thiruvananthapuram. The more enlightened Maharajas in India had the wit to safeguard the best interests of their citizens. However, with the re-organisation of the States in 1958 under the language theme, Malabar became part of the new State of Kerala, where the Malayalam language prevailed. The Princely states of Kochi and Thiruvananthapuram acceded; new ideas travelled fast.

I attended two family weddings in my childhood and youth; the first was of my father's niece in 1948. She was the daughter of his widowed sister and therefore his responsibility. The ceremony took all of five minutes, and because it was just after the war and rice-rationing was severe, households were allowed only a half gunny-bag of rice for a wedding, about fifteen kilograms. So, a very austere event indeed.

We were supposed to invite close family only, but the entire neighbourhood turned up, invited or not. There was a tacit understanding that people who lived near would come anyway but leave discreetly before the feast was served. The bridegroom's party took precedence and the number that he could bring with him would have been negotiated earlier. Our saviour, my aunt who was married to a farmer, would quietly disobey every rule in the book and send some rice to us. She would send it in a large basket, with coconuts and jack fruit, and camouflaged under old cloth, on the head of one of her maids. If my father knew about this, he would have been outraged: he considered himself (and by extension, all his family) absolutely law-abiding. So, when the maid brought the rice, Ammamma had to make sure Achan was nowhere in the vicinity.

In better days a minimum of two desserts would have been served at a middle-class wedding, one with rice and milk, and one with banana and jaggery. With austerity, there was just one served, that too a wheat *Payasam*. Wheat was what we were given on our ration cards to supplement the rice, so whether we liked it or not wheat was what was served. Textiles were also in short supply, so the bride had a limited trousseau. Just returned from jail anyway, I doubt my father could have afforded a rich trousseau.

When I got married in 1957, the ceremony was still threadbare. In my case the show moved from inside the house to a *panthal* (tent) outside, because my father, by that time a well-known politician, had too many people he felt obliged to invite. When the labourers brought cartloads of thatch and bamboo poles, the whole road would know that the house was gearing up for a big event. As the *panthal* slowly went up in front of the veranda in the yard, it would cut off the sunlight to some extent, and it would become just another big, appended room. This is where the ceremony would be conducted, and later, it would be laid out with grass mats with banana leaves in front, for the male guests to eat. Women would eat inside

I tried to rein my father in when I noticed the preparations, because I knew he couldn't really afford this big show. *'Let's just have a few invitees, let's not buy all this gold for me; after all I managed to get to age twenty-two with very little,'* I suggested. He insisted that he had been to so many weddings in Thalassery, and this was his only chance to return that hospitality, because he had no other children but me. *'They will come, all of them, eat the wedding sadhya (feast) and go away complaining of too little salt in the Sambar or not enough sugar in the payasam,'* I argued. *And you will be bankrupt.* And so he was.

The ritual was mercifully short. An exchange of jasmine garlands in front of the nilavilakku, a momentary chant from the *pujari*, an overpowering smell of hot coconut oil, sandalwood and jasmine, and three times round the lamp holding hands. Now you're single, now you're not! I remember the broad jasmine garland mounted on a frame at the neck-end was heavy round my shoulder; I smothered a giant sneeze. The holding hands with a total stranger made me uncomfortable too. I didn't manage a look at his face because I kept my head down like brides were supposed to do.

I couldn't see my father anywhere near. So many other faces, but not he. *'Where are you? Are you watching all this? Are you keeping track?'*

34

4

When I was about fourteen years old, my father decided my school was just not doing enough; there was so much the school could not teach me. it was part of his mission to fill that gap, to educate, improve, and generally make me fit to manage the twentieth century, (and totally unfit to marry a local Nair man). I resisted that mission vigorously when he was not looking; I just wanted to be like all the other girls around, relaxed, uneducated man-fodder.

One of his original ideas was to train me to speak fluently and lucidly in public, in both Malayalam and English. On a lazy Sunday morning when I should be picking green mangoes from the compound behind our house, he would summon me.

The lesson would begin on the front veranda of our house -- one prong of a many-pronged attack. This involved me standing six metres from him, on our walkway to the front-gate, and speaking on a topic he would set. He would stand on the veranda and instruct. I had five minutes to prepare. He was a demanding teacher, teaching me to 'throw' my voice, slow down, look at him, not mumble... Topics included Freedom, Non-violence, Books I liked and why...

Father dictated what I read and supervised that process. When I finished reading a book he had instructed me to read, I had to do a little review in a note-book and show it to him. I often tried to copy the blurb at the back, but he found me out very quickly. 'I am not looking for second-hand opinions,' he said. 'I want you to think for yourself – not trust others.'

With poetry, he was more demanding. I had to memorise four lines of the book of that week and recite it to him. *Karuna* by Kumaran Ashan was his favourite. Karuna was the story of *Vasavadatha,* a beautiful prostitute in Madhura. I enjoyed that story in verse; she sounded feisty. *In Memoriam* was another matter. For the rest of my life I have kept a safe distance from Tennyson, including the bewildering Lady of Shalott.

Interestingly my reading speed in both Malayalam and English grew exponentially, and my memory blotted up anything that came along, without discrimination.

Our walkway was a public place, and when I had to perform, passers-by would stare. For an audience, I generally had the crows on the coconut tree, the ownerless cats going from house to house at the time the fish parted with their heads each morning, and two or three children from around the neighbourhood, who would stand and gape at this unusual girl and her even more unusual father. I hated all of this, but there was no escape. In school and college later, however, I became the star debater.

My father enticed me into his activities (all except swimming) and now, in my eighties, I find I have a variety of diversions to call upon when time hangs heavily, and I am looking to escape my writing, I have a large savings account of varied activities that I have banked, under duress, for my old age. Not to mention a greedy reading speed.

Gardening, which is a favourite occupation of mine, works every time. Though, at the time, I joined in reluctantly. Achan usually planted red spinach, green spinach, aubergine, beans and okra. There were also the climbing beans (*mange tout*), the centrepiece of the garden. He and his best friend had an ongoing competition about whose beans did the best each year.

My father would send me out to water the vegetable-patch every evening in the summer. Water had to be drawn from the well and carried in pots to the garden in front of the house. I was supposed to join the young boy who was our gofer, as it wouldn't be fair to expect him to do it all on his own; also, I had to spend hours weeding with him, when I would rather just be. I was a teenager then, but Achan made no concessions to the alternate world of teens, which my granddaughter, Asha, now inhabits with such panache.

I would hitch up my ankle-length skirt, along with my reluctance and draw water from our well, tugging at the rope-and-pulley system. Physical exertion was meant to be ennobling! But, all it did for me was drench me from waist down. My skirt would start getting entangled in my legs; periodically, I would need to stop and wring out the water from the bottom of it. Neighbours and family looked on in astonishment in those years at this father-and-daughter team; in those years girls were not meant to be going everywhere with their fathers. And fathers, as the alpha males in the house, were not meant to take any notice of daughters. Also, digging, weeding, watering, were not occupations of middle-class females. You had maids and helpers for that, didn't you? What was *Vakil's* (lawyer's) daughter doing, joining in with the garden-boy?

The garden boy, was a priceless urchin. He could disappear into thin air if he heard my father's footsteps approaching, with what he imagined was instructions about the watering. I knew where to find him though he changed his hidey-holes on a regular basis.

'Don't want to get your skirt wet, do you?' he'd ask innocently. 'We could do it early tomorrow morning before your bath.'

There were in fact a few rules in our house regarding house-boys. No shouting at them and don't ask them to do anything you are not willing to do yourself. If they were young they had to be fed when the children of the house were fed. I believe my father adopted all of this from Mahatma Gandhi; in practice the women who ran the kitchen ignored my father with impunity because he never went anywhere near the kitchen.

5

My mother got married when she was fifteen, I was born when she was sixteen, and she died at eighteen, after giving birth to another girl, who survived her by ten days. Penicillin arrived in Thalassery only in 1949; it saved my father's life when he had pneumonia that year, but it came too late for my mother, who contracted tuberculosis when she was seventeen years old. Indeed, in 1949, the doctor who treated my father with Penicillin took pains to warn the household that this was a new drug and he was taking a chance!

As I grew older, I became curious about this child-mother of mine. Was she beautiful, loving, intelligent? Did I look like her? But information was difficult to extract from anybody. My father never mentioned her. Still, I persevered and picked up titbits. Not enough to form a whole picture, but fragments that pinged briefly in my head.

In her husband's home, I was told, my mother was treated like the child she was, instructed by her mother-in-law when to eat, bathe, do housework etc. If she had not washed her feet, last thing before she went to bed, my father would scold her and send her back downstairs to the bathroom.

Her hair was lank and uncared for when she came to her husband's home. Achamma, apparently, put coconut oil on her hair and brushed it by hand daily, until it grew luxurious and long. Thick, long hair, was a sign of beauty in Malayalee girls and Achamma was not going to let her son's bride lose out in this respect.

From asking the extended family of my father and mother, visitors who came and went, like Achan's best friend's wife, I garnered snippets of information about this young person. They had been young brides together, from the same village, married to two young lawyers, at the same time, had their first children the same year.

My mother's footprints seemed light and insubstantial. 'She was clever with numbers,' they said. 'That's why you are good at Maths.' Also, she adored your father and he treated her with much affection and little respect.'

My father did not respond kindly to my queries about my mother, either. 'She was clever. Very loving. No, you don't look like her at all.' Not much there. There were no photographs of her decorating the walls; even my grandmother in Madras, her mother, did not have any. It was not a time when people owned cameras or took photographs. There was just one sepia shot of her with a group of lawyers and their wives in an annual lawyers' get-together, which my father kept in the bottom drawer of his chest-of-drawers, along with a pencil drawing of her, enlarged from that sepia shot. She was wearing a sari on the wrong shoulder and looked somewhat out of place. I got a brief glimpse once when he was organising his chest of drawers.

When I asked my Ammamma, she said my mother did not own a sari, never wore one, and did not know how to drape it. She normally wore a white mundu, (a cloth round the waist,) a blouse and top-cloth *(veshti)* like all the other women in the house. For the occasion of the party, she had borrowed a sari from her sister-in-law.

These days, girls of her age – fifteen – in India, wear short skirts and tops just like the western girls they see in films and magazines. They wouldn't dare hitch up their skirts the way school-girls do now-a-days in England; that will take another year or two. My daughter takes a good look every morning to see what Asha, my granddaughter, is up to with her uniform-skirt. I suspect, it alters its drop some time on the way to school. I don't blame Asha – all her classmates are doing the same thing.

Achachan, (paternal grandfather) apparently, would feel sorry for my mother when he saw her playing childhood games with stones, with my cousin, Appu, who was then ten years old. But then, Achamma, was eleven years old when she got married, so there was no great empathy for my child-mother's plight. Achachan, I was told, would secrete penny-sweets in his shirt-pocket and sneak them to her when he returned from his walks, and she adored him. He died a month before her when she was in hospital in Madras, having her second baby, and they never told her.

I escaped an early marriage because my father never recovered from the guilt of marrying an innocent child. In my teens I often heard him say to friends and elders who brought proposals of marriage for me, 'She is going to marry late, may be after she is twenty-five.' I got close.

My father never remarried, neither would he hand

me over to his in-laws to bring up. This would have been normal practice at that time. My Velyamma (maternal grandmother), was still young, and had already given birth to seven children, and would have another four before she called it a day. One daughter of hers was only seven months older than me, and another was born when I was two years old. One more child would have been absorbed into that family without being noticed – it was a loving family that always had endless time for children, theirs or others.

My father decided to bring me up on his own – even his sisters who ran his household later on did not have much say in it. I slept in his bed; he inspected my feet and my teeth daily before I got into bed. After my morning bath he would feel the hair at the nape of my neck to check whether I had washed it properly. As late as 1952, when I was in the second year of my pre-degree studies (then called Intermediate), he was supervising my morning hygiene. If my hair felt dry he would know my bath had been quick and careless; I would have to do it all over again.

If I scratched my head a lot, which I did often, I was summarily sent to his sister with instructions that every last louse and nit had to come off. Ammamma would cluck and swear and take out her instruments of torture. The *eereli* especially, the long wooden fork-like object was the chief instrument of torture. The tines at the end were about two inches in length, you had to clutch the strands of hair near the roots with it and pull, not very gently, to draw the nits out. A little like the electric curlers of now-a-days. Lice were comparatively easy – they tumbled out, and it was great fun to put them on one thumb and squash them with the other, with a satisfying plop.

Achan took his parenting seriously, it seemed, annoying the women in the house by taking over duties that they considered their domain, including my manicure and pedicure, if you can call chopping off nails with a pair of shaving scissors those fancy names.

Sometimes, many years later, my father would often be discussing his brief with a group of clients in his office on one side of the house, when I sneaked out past his door on my way to college. '*No flowers in the hair today?*' he would call out smiling, and I would hear his pride in me, in his voice.

All of us girls grew our hair as long as we could. Mine was thick and luxurious, well below my waist by the time I was eighteen years old, and I would wear it in a long heavy plait. In Kerala, the two bench-marks of good looks were long, black hair and a fair ('wheatish') complexion. To this day, if you look in the Matrimonial Pages of newspapers, the marriage advertisements highlight this predilection for fairness. Many of the families, who have a man in the house looking for a bride, put a proviso in the advertisement that the girl should be fair or of *wheatish* complexion. And of course, there is the popularity of skin lightening creams.

I was fair by South Indian standards and vain as they come. So, I always decorated my long plait with flowers. I didn't spend a great deal of time in front of mirrors as there were no mirrors in our house, except my father's small shaving one, which was the size of a Kindle. We washed our hair daily and stood out in the sun to dry it, slowly, sensuously, passing our fingers through it. Indeed, I have never in my life owned a hair-dryer.

After our hair dried, we looked for flowers. If we had run out of flowers in our compound, the next-door house would give us some. There were the pink-and-white *Yeshoda*, and deep orange *Kanakambaram* blooms, growing on fences in our plush green neighbourhood, to make into garlands if jasmine was exhausted. College lectures began at ten in the morning, so there was plenty of time to indulge our narcissism. However, we were not allowed to wash our hair or wear flowers during our periods, and my father's happy query would sometimes be too embarrassing to answer.

My periods, when they started, was the one watershed moment when the women-folk tried to claim their girl – and lost the battle. Achan swatted them away.

'Must make sweets for distribution to our neighbours,' my aunt declared. 'It is the custom.' Clearly, a girl becoming a woman was good news that all neighbours should be informed about, though I wanted to hug that knowledge to myself. Achan gave her five rupees for the purpose. She bought coconut oil, *vellam* (blocks of unrefined brown sugar), and over-ripe bananas, and set about making our traditional sweet for all feast days – *Thandilamrithu*. Oily, round and rich, just the way I liked.

Women from neighbouring houses came visiting one after the other, bearing *Kalathappam* and *Unda*, both sweets made from rice and sugar or jaggery.

Ammamma instructed me not to bathe for three days. I was also not allowed to enter the kitchen or the puja room; I should not go within the vicinity of any man because it was thought the force-field of a woman during her periods would be toxic to him. I was relegated to the back-veranda.

This was common practice. When I went to my *Velyamma's* (maternal grandmother) house on the far side of town, near the Thiruvangad temple, or my aunt's house in the village, I was obliged to observe all the segregations that went with the territory. This was not entirely a penance as we would be excused from the chores around the house, as we were not allowed into most of the rooms including the kitchen. My mother's sister, Thankamani, and I always had cartloads of gossip to tell each other, mainly about boys and the romances that sprang up in our schools. Sometimes, Thankamani and I would pretend to have periods together as this gave us a great deal of us-time. Velyamma, I suspect, was not entirely fooled, but how was she to check?

During that first period, Achan came upon me skulking around in the back-veranda, banished as I was from the house.

'Mmm?' he asked. He was on his way upstairs from the latrine.

'I am not to touch anything today,' I offered, a little embarrassed.

'Bathed?'

'Velyamma said I can't bathe till day-after-tomorrow.'

Achan looked sharply at me and exploded.

'You bathe daily. Unless you are ill. And this is not ill.'

'She is unclean. Mustn't touch anyone. She should take a day off from school,' Velyamma insisted, from somewhere behind the kitchen door. Velyamma always spoke to my father from behind a door, ready to disappear if the dialogue went awry.

Achan tossed his head. 'Nonsense,' he said loudly, as he went up the stairs. Nonsense was a favourite word of his when he came face to face with the old customs and superstitions. But he gave me a pat on my head before he disappeared. Co-conspirators, as usual.

The women did not make any claims thereafter until years later, when I went home for my first confinement. They muttered and murmured without any hope of being heard. However, it is worth mentioning that it was Velyamma who initiated me into the mysteries of periods and comforted me with hot tea and a pillow over my stomach (our substitute for a hot water bottle) when the cramps came. She also found the soft rags that I could use to manage the flow. Sanitary pads and I came to know each other only when I had left India for good after I got married and started living in Colombo.

6

There were always other children in our extended household. My father's spinster sister presided over the kitchen. All the children in the house called her Ammamma, and the adults called her Edayi, which had been her nickname from youth. She was the closest to a surrogate mother I ever had, and when my father was not around, I slept with her.

Achan's widowed sister's daughter, Naani, who was seven years older than me, carried me around on her hip from the time she was ten years old. I called her Naani Edathy. Naani was unusually fair for a South Indian girl, and had huge, black eyes, with long lashes that seemed to curl at the ends. She would have been beautiful, if not for her front teeth, which overlapped, so that she could never quite close her mouth. When she laughed she would hide her smile behind her palm and I would feel a great sense of pity for her.

When I went to her with my little sorrows, and there were many, she would take my hurts away with her tenderness. I was prone to grazes, scratches and boils and capitalised on them fully for sympathy, crystallised sugar and grated coconut. The sugar was stored in an old Ovaltine tin, on top of the kitchen lintel, which I couldn't quite reach. Naani would sneak a little out for me to pacify me; with coconut it was gourmet stuff.

When I was six and she, thirteen, she was still carting me about, listing slightly to the hip on which I was perched; she had short legs, and I would dangle from her hips, my feet not far from the ground. I remember that smell of shallots she carried with her, because her first job, every day after breakfast was peeling shallots for lunch.

She was the person I adored, who bathed me when I was little and told me stories from *Ramayanam* and *Mahabaratham*, our epics. When she brushed my hair with the old comb, which had lost most of its tines, I could feel her love in those tines. I loved her also because she was the only other person who had lice in her hair like me, so I was not completely alone. And she had infinite patience with all my needs.

In that extended household, people came and went. After all, if one man in the village lived in town and made good, he was everyone's property. Especially if there was no wife to moderate events. There were my father's nephews who came from the village; sometimes they stayed a year or two, at other times they came for a day or a week. I was used to this random traffic; they were normally fed and watered by the womenfolk. In old age, my father's nephews would be responsible for looking after him. He could call upon them as a matter of right. Though the laws had changed, old customs prevailed. When I was living in England in the seventies and eighties, it was these nephews who cared for him.

My Velyachan, (my father's brother) at that time (in the thirties and forties) a doctor in Penang, sent his son, Appu, to go to school in Thalassery.

48

Velyachan lived on a rubber estate in Malaysia, and the only school there was a ramshackle affair for the children of the labourers, mainly Tamils who had emigrated from India, in the days when, India, Malaysia and Ceylon had no hard borders, as all three belonged to Britain, so people went back and forth without documents. A trip by steamer took two weeks and people who went to Malaysia in search of fortune came home rarely. The Tamil labourers never came back to India. They settled in Malaysia, and in Ceylon (now Sri Lanka) and became the persecuted minority in that country.

So Appu, whom I called Appu ettan (elder brother), he being four years older than me, and very conscious of his seniority as well as his familial ascendancy, being a boy in a mainly female household, came to live with us to go to school in India. He went away sometimes for months but always came back; something of a perennial. His younger sister, Mani, a few months older than me came to live with us in 1940. I did not call her Mani Edathy (elder sister), but we girls became a partnership in our household.

It was just before the war in Malaysia started that velyachan sent his children to Thalassery out of harm's way. They came suddenly, with two young uncles, who were also returning to India, having lived all their lives in Malaysia.

With Mani's coming, my status as a lone child was cancelled. Until the war ended and her parents came to claim her and Appuettan.

Appu and Mani stayed with us for six years until I was eleven years old. Velyachan, my father's beloved only brother who had been caught in the war in Malaysia, returned; the war was over. A few months before, we had the first bit of news from him.

A radio message was picked up by some kind spirit in Madras and forwarded to us in a telegram.

Both of us safe. Anxious mother's health, it said. I am amazed I remember the exact wording of that text. Achamma had died some years earlier, and I was deeply sad for him, that he would come back to that fact. We had no means of contacting him and it took almost another six months for him to come home. They had lost everything they owned in the war and had to save up again to pay for their journey to India by steamer. So, they came only in the spring of 1946.

They brought with them crisp, new Japanese currency, which was now totally worthless. Mani and I invented games, setting up shops, selling imaginary cigarettes and matches, exchanging Japanese money. We created a cattle market, making cattle shapes with Jack-fruit leaves. Velyamma, (uncle's wife) brought swathes of parachute silk – manna from heaven for our household, which was struggling to clothe everyone. Textiles were severely rationed and the black market flourished in this as in everything else in short supply: rice, kerosene, cloth, sugar... Naani made blouses from that silk and added trimmings to brighten that uniform cream colour.

When they returned to India Mani's parents stayed with us for a few weeks, picked up their children, and left. I was gobsmacked. I didn't know adults could do this – make decisions that changed our lives, without saying a word to us. I missed Mani and life returned to single-child country.

After this decisive separation, Mani came back very occasionally for holidays, looking more polished, well-dressed and cow-licked than I could aspire to be. I continued my *mofussil* (little community) existence without too many trimmings in clothes or attitudes.

I missed Mani when she was not around. To this day, when we are both cranky octogenarians, Mani and I like to touch base often, she in Kochi and I in Purley. Father took all these goings and comings in his stride; he adored his brother anyway. He often said that he missed those two children he had looked after and loved for six years.

Achan had so much love in him, he drew people to himself like moths to a light. Most were good people, but occasionally he would attract a scoundrel or a liar; I would recognise the rot beneath the surface of the person who was exploiting his affections. Once I warned him about a man who kept 'borrowing' small amount of money from him. He said,

'If a hundred rupees is all it takes to separate wheat from chaff, then that hundred is well-spent.'

As the one educated person from his family, my father was expected to educate and sustain whichever child presented itself on the doorstep; indeed he hardly noticed them. All of us ate the ubiquitous moong-dhal and *conjee* morning and evening and *Sambhar* -- that watery, catch-all vegetable curry -- and rice in the afternoon, with a little fish to taste if we were lucky. People slept in corridors on mats. My father's house-rules were clear: all the children should be treated equally, no favouritism.

If the visitors were adult and male they became *ettans* and females became *echis*. If they were family, defined fairly generously, they could come indoors and into the kitchen and sit around inside the house. If not, they sat on the bench on the veranda; Ammamma would deal with them. As in 'How are you? And what news in the village?' She would serve lunch to them and see them on their way.

Many of the visitors dropped in for a quick lunch if they had business in the Civil Courts near our house. The new Land Ownership legislation transferring inheritance of land to the children of owners rather than nephews and nieces, precipitated many land disputes and the litigation increased in volume. The whole idea of your children inheriting your assets was a huge realignment of attitudes. Even after this happened, the parents continued to carry a visceral responsibility towards their nephews and nieces that they could not shake off.

7

After Mani went away, my father took me along with him whenever he went out of the house in the evening, till I personally signed out at about fourteen, because his daily haunts, the Cosmopolitan Club, where he played billiards, and the local beach where he went walking, eventually bored me. His men-friends, however, got used to this little girl, Raghavan's little lamb, who was the only child in their man-world.

Once I even tagged along to a hospital, eight miles away, where he was interrogating a client, who had been knifed by the violent wing of the local Communists, in a political vendetta. These were the years when the Maoist Naxalite wing of the Communists assassinated many landowners, set fire to barns and buildings, and raided police stations to walk away with the weapons inside. The victim lay on an iron bed surrounded by family. He had crepe bandages going around his chest, and they were sodden with dark blood. The nurse attending to him peeled off the bandage to show my father the extent of his wounds. The man also had a huge gash on his shoulders and another deep one on his back. I remember the sight of the wounds upset me deeply – this was perhaps one place my father should not have taken me, because it gave me nightmares for weeks afterwards.

Achan became Public Prosecutor in 1949 and he was inundated with cases involving communist violence against landowners and civil society. Threats against his life became commonplace; the Naxalites did not like the level of success he was attaining in putting away the perpetrators of violence against the State.

The threats terrified me. When he went to party-meetings out of town, I didn't go with him, because he would come home very late, at one or two the next morning. Transport in those days was uncertain and no schedule was adhered to, especially after dark. So, I would sit up till he came home, with my heart in my mouth.

Eventually the police gave him a small revolver and a packet of bullets for self-defence.

'I don't know one end of this object from the other,' he said.

'Just keep it. Merely waving it will scare them away.'

'Scares *me*,' my father said. He picked it up gingerly, like a dead lizard, and dropped it into the top drawer of his chest-of-drawers. It stayed there for many years; it never got loaded.

After that a policeman was posted at our house for security at night. Ammamma fed him tea; gave him a blanket and a mat. I would hear him urinating copiously on the trunk of the coconut tree next to Achan's office, though the toilet was only a metre away. He slept on the parapet of our veranda and disappeared in the morning before anyone got up. After a few months a torch from the window-sill also disappeared.

When we couldn't find it, we assumed one of the beggars might have walked off with it.

'No, I used it yesterday,' our houseboy said. 'And the beggars have not come today.'

Achan was quite sanguine about the whole incident.

'I think the policeman is entitled to a torch after all these months.' He smiled. 'Policemen's salaries are very small. We should leave an umbrella out for him as well. For when he needs to urinate.'

So Achan hung an old umbrella on the loose beam on the eaves. But the umbrella survived.

The defendants' lawyer on the Naxalite side was Krishna Iyer, who made a name for himself as a Supreme Court Justice in later years. These two men were good friends and had a natural respect for each other as people who were well-read and forward-looking in a subsistence society. Every time Krishna Iyer came to Thalassery, he would visit our house, and when he left again to go to Delhi, he was tearful.

'This may be the last time we see each other,' he would moan.

In the end Iyer lived well into his nineties, long after my father died. When I went to Kochi a few years after, I visited Krishna Iyer in his office, where he received a procession of visitors daily, who came with various requests. I waited my turn and went inside after a long wait.

'I don't want anything from you,' I said. I could see from his face he was expecting another person with a sob-story. I told him I came out of nostalgia, and he was kind and asked after my family. But he was also very busy.

'You must come again,' he said. I never did.

His secretary saw me out.

'I used to work for your father for some years,' he said. 'He was a very special man. After you got married and went away he used to tell me about you and your boys. He was proud of you.' The clerk made me cry.

Not many men wasted time on abstractions and reading in those days, especially English books, and this was the link between the two lawyers.

Hanging was still prevalent in the early fifties if you were found guilty of murder, and many communists must have ended that way. My father did not believe in hanging – he did not trust justice to be always correct and hanging was irreversible. What if the judgment was wrong? He would mutter and murmur inconclusively about this, making me uneasy. When a case was drawing to a conclusion, and it appeared the accused would be executed, my father was unhappy. 'This is not humane,' he would insist.

When Achan played Billiards at The Cosmopolitan Club, I could sit on the high bench in the corner and watch so long as I kept perfectly still and quiet. When I tired of this I would go to the huge main hall and look at the magazines on the card table. I read the Life Magazine, Punch, The Illustrated Weekly of India, The Week and many others, which were scattered in an untidy heap on the baize surface of the card table. Achan would stay late sometimes, the men would order *Biriyani* and I would eat with them. As a Hindu I was not supposed to eat beef, so one day I asked Achan about this.

'Who says? Whose rules are these? Make your

own rules. If you can eat lamb, and chicken... Think about it.'

However, I knew enough not to mention this beef-eating to the women at home. Later in life, when I was faced with the many ways I should or should not behave, the dos and the don'ts, as a Hindu, I always fell back on my father's instruction: think, make up your own mind. At some point, around the age of twenty-five, when I started working in Nigeria, and came across people of many faiths and beliefs, I gave up on religion. Totally. Including Hinduism. I didn't see the point.

As I grew older, I enjoyed the walks on our small *maidanam* near the house more than going to the club. The little beach, which was known as *Cheriya Maidanam* (small green) as against the large one in town, was a five-minute walk from where we lived. The sea was just a hop, step and a jump away, down the rocks on the edge, where the waves on a good day, would splash you wet, as they fought the rocks.

The sea ate away at those rocks and the land receded. The town council heaped huge concrete boulders in the area where the sea was most destructive. I remember a time when my father could wade and swim far away into the sea, so far that I had to strain to see his head, bobbing with the waves. The sea had claimed half a mile of land in the four decades I had been in Africa and the United Kingdom.

As I grew older and more venturesome, I would sit on the promontory, on the rocks at the far end of the beach, from where I could watch the sun slowly descending into the Arabian Sea, in a blaze of oranges and pinks, until that final moment, when it went under quite suddenly, as though it had given up the battle.

Today, the green where I sat and dreamt has been walled off and a park has come up in that space. Many potted plants adorn the sides of the walkways between the greenery, and loud *filmi* music blares from loudspeakers. What a desecration!

Behind me and across the road are the Civil Courts, their tennis courts where my father sometimes played, and the Bar Association library quite near the main road. The buildings have been renovated, and a large photo of my father hangs on the wall of the lounge -- he had been the President of the Bar Association for a few years. It is a prim picture of him, none of the mischief showing. He would probably say he looks like one of the tax dodgers he defended at some point, and I can hear myself agreeing.

Sometimes my father's friend, Ernest, would come with us to the beach, bringing his daughters Mabel, and Ida with him. Ernest was a lawyer of the same generation as my father and lived on Court Road. He was a Mathematician before he became a lawyer and would point out interesting Maths facts to me while we walked home in the half-light of the stars.

I loved going to the beach with Mabel and Ida, and those two girls became a permanent part of my life in Thalassery. When we went to school we shared a *jutka (horse-drawn carriage)*, and later, when we were older, we walked to school and college together. Amazingly, we still keep in touch, Mabel in Kozhikode, not far from where we were both born, and I in distant Purley, in England. I have lost touch with Ida, but Mabel still sounds the same, looks pretty much, agelessly, the same, and is still the mild-mannered, kind girl she always was.

People around my father got used to this child-appendage of his, and I got used to dealing with the polite, inconsequential queries of his men-friends. 'You like to go everywhere with your father, eh?' An answer was not required. Over a long period, I perfected a polite smile.

I was growing up fast; now I preferred to stay at home, listening to Radio Ceylon, which had a programme called *Binaca Geethmala*, (literally, a song- stream) uninterrupted *filmi* music, interspersed with advertisements for Binaca tooth-paste, for three long evening hours. I was that kind of age. If you walked down the road where we lived, you could hear the Geethmala blaring in one house after another, fading and flaring as you went past.

The parapet on our balcony was my retreat -- if I did not put the lights on, I could sit there, day-dream, think, contemplate the world according to Lin Yutang, Bertrand Russell or C E M Joad, all philosophers my father had inflicted on me, when I was about fourteen years old, and whom I could just about understand now.

The paddy fields stretched away on three sides of our compound, looking inexplicably pink and green: the muddy waters were pink and the young paddy shoots a gentle green. The frogs croaked, the crickets buzzed, and I learned to be on my own for long stretches of time, living in my mind and weighing up my world.

At harvest and planting seasons there was the song of the women labourers singing out stories of old chiefs and male warriors. There was a man in charge there too; they called him *mesthri (master)*. He would come in the evenings to check how much work the women had done in the day and pay them. It was an open secret that one of those women was his mistress and she had a son by him. As a woman of the working class she had much more personal freedom than someone like me; there was no scandal attached and she could do pretty much what she wanted. In fact, I suspected, she rather enjoyed the special status bestowed on her by the mesthri. The community called her son *Pirakatha Mone*, meaning the son who was not born. All children born out of wedlock were called this non-name by the community.

The women came to our house in the afternoons for the starchy, *conjee* water, which Ammamma saved for them; if they saw me watching them they would change their song at work to tease me and sing about girls ready for marriage.

8

Father, however, in spite of his busy career as one of the leading criminal lawyers in Thalassery, did not give up on his Pygmalion mission. I was his Eliza Doolittle. He set work for me every week: memorising English and Malayalam poetry, reading the poems of Vallathol, and Kalidasan's *Shakunthalam* in translation. I hated some of it: Romain Rolland in stilted English was not a favourite. For the rest of my life I kept a safe distance from Tennyson and Rolland. Strangely enough I took to *The Baghavad Gita* and The King James Bible, The Complete Works of Bernard Shaw, which I loved, and Aldous Huxley's *Brave New World*, which made me think about where the world was heading. When my father gave me books to read, I often found that they were well-beyond my comprehension. Gandhi's *Experiments with Truth*, for instance, in English as well as its Malayalam translation, both equally turgid, impenetrable– what was he getting at?

Then there were the early morning walks, early as in five in the morning, by the Koduvalli river when I was allowed to talk to him only in English. I can still hear his voice, chasing me out of bed, '*Do not waste precious early morning hours.*' Ammamma would make us black coffee laced with ghee and lots of sugar. This routine made me fluent in English early in life, so much so, that if he wanted to say something to me that the rest of the house should not hear, he spoke in English.

There was also the blessed *charkha* – Gandhi's charkha. It was a flimsy contraption, made of wood, with a large wheel at one end, wherein you fed a 'sliver' of cotton wool and a thin thread of white cotton came out at the other. I wasn't very good at this, being naturally ham-fisted at anything remotely related to sewing or thread. And this was not something my father could teach me, thank God.

This was the material from which *Khadar* was made – the Indian-made cloth, which had nothing to do with the Lancashire mills. This was Gandhi's answer to the fact that the British were taking our raw cotton away to England, and it came back as cloth, which was many times the price of cotton made in India, and it destroyed a flourishing cottage-industry. The whole *Swaraj* (Own Country) movement knew about the Bengal muslin industry, famous for the quality of its material, that had been similarly destroyed by the colonial masters. The weavers had been forbidden from weaving, their looms destroyed, and in a few cases, their thumbs chopped off.

Was this kind of protest, boycotting foreign cloth, effective? I doubt that it bothered the Lancashire Mills. But it was good propaganda; it was something individuals could do without resorting to violence, and it was a powerful statement of solidarity with the objectives of the Independence movement. Interestingly, the textile industry expanded and became a strong earner a few years from the end of the British rule. Today, handlooms flourish in India and the textiles come at many different prices, making them accessible to rich and poor alike. The colours and designs are amazing; they reflect the old mango and temple designs as well as the new modern geometric and psychedelic patterns. There is no end to the creativity in this sector.

My father's self-imposed brief encompassed me in many ways. He would take me to the Metropole Hotel in town for breakfast, on our way back from our walk, and order non-Indian food, insisting I learn how to eat with fork and knife. In this he was not successful; I liked eating with my hands. Still do.

One morning, at the end of our walk, he detoured off to the Catholic Church next to the St Joseph's Boys' Secondary School. We smelled the sea right at the entrance, so we walked down to the ancient, mossy, slippery steps at the back of the school. The sea stretched out in front of us, and in the distance, I could see the small *maidanam*, which was near our house, and the promontory on which I sat to nurture my dreams. The waves lashed the steps – it felt good to stand there and let the sea talk to us.

Later I went inside the chapel, bent my knees in front of the door as I entered, and made my way to the holy water font, shaped like a large half-shell, on the side-wall. I dipped my fingers and made the sign of the cross, bowing my head when I said, *Jesus*, as I had been taught at my school. I was impressed with the open-door policy of this religion, such that a pagan like me could slip in and do obeisance and walk out. Many years later, in Finchley, I went looking for a church to absorb the peace that such places offer, but the doors were firmly closed. With good reason: I heard the silver was being systematically thieved from church premises, so they had to lock doors to wayward visitors like me. The church in India would not have possessed anything worth taking away, except perhaps the whiff of sanctimony, which priests seemed to carry on their floating habits.

My father waited at the door for me and grinned as I went towards him.

'You look as though you've been here before,' he said.

'We come across with the Sisters on feast days,' I said.

My Religious Education was carried on over many morning walks. The Protestant church, also in the middle of Thalasserry town, was not open early in the morning. It did not have the presence of the chapel, placed as it was, a few metres from the noisy main road. The first time I went inside was when I was twenty years old, to attend the wedding of my friend, Mabel.

The local mosque in the Big Maidanam, did not allow women in, for worship or for anything else. It was a small building and I peeked from outside into the large hall of prayers. It had green painted windows and minaret and men wandered in and out as I watched. The huge Bo tree in the maidanam was within a few metres, and Achan and I sat under it, early one morning; Achan wanted me to listen to the muezzin's call to prayer.

That call was a stirring invocation; at that time, I did not understand why. Today, I know that it distils all the sorrows of the world and I find it unbearable sometimes. The church bells cannot hold a candle to that summons. The microphones have not improved it. As Graham Greene insisted, this combination of old religion and new technology simply cannot go together. Though *he* opted for the old religion anyway.

In Kochi, where I lived for a while, I would hear the mosque the other side of the backwaters, along which my house nestled, first, at turn-over-and-go-to-sleep time in the morning. The call completed, the temple, also across the river, would come on, as though in competition.

Achan took me to the Jewish synagogue and explained their rituals and beliefs to me. Somewhere along the line, he also told me he never went to temples, and preferred not to practise any religion. I have always wondered whether he was responsible for me becoming an agnostic. Or was it all that indiscriminate reading?

Educating me cannot have been easy, I had my own pastimes: going next door to watch their goats giving birth and the hens roosting, picking the fallen tamarind fruit of the ginormous, tamarind tree in their vast garden, building houses of cards with the second-hand, dog-eared pack my father and his friends had finished playing '*Twenty-eight*' with...

But Achan was obstinate. He even went so far as to decide that he had to introduce me to South Indian classical music, the kind he sang out of tune in the bathroom and going up the stairs to his room. When we got electricity on our road sometime after Independence, he was the first house-holder to get a connection. We got points only in three rooms in the house to keep the cost within reason. Soon he bought himself a big brown Bakelite Philips radio.

Every morning he would tune in to All India Radio, *Kozhikode,* to listen to *Udayageetham,* (morning song) really loud. I had no choice but to listen. His favourite was *Vaadaapi Ganapathe,* a lyric in praise of the elephant god, *Ganapathy,* and soon I was humming it even more out of tune than he. At that time, I didn't like classical south Indian music at all, following the herd as I did, listening to Hindi *filmi* music whenever I got the chance. Those were the days of Saigal *(Suhani raath)* and his music was humming in everyone's head.

My father converted me explaining the *thaalams* (beats) to me, starting with *Aadi* and *Roopaka.* Amazingly, in a few months, I was hooked. Filmi music was still pleasant, but no more than just pleasant. Carnatic music became an addiction. Today, when I am in India, I pick up the CDs of classical music from the south and the north of India; this was a gift a very special father gave to me.

And what a gift! I knew then that the music that you never listen to because you are ignorant about it, can still draw you in. So I spent hours in my teens trying to tune into Radio London. The reception was poor, but one day, Terry Wogan popped up; his voice was like smooth vermicelli *payasam.* Another day, I came upon Gregorian Chants – and got 'converted' to church music.

Much later, in Nigeria, I would listen to the Sacred Heart Irish nuns singing Easter hymns, in the Training college in Enugu, where I worked, and it was like meeting up with an old friend. During Lent all the Sisters, the teachers and students would go to the chapel to practise their hymns. I was the only non-Catholic in the place; the staff room and the corridors of the college would be silent, and the music wafted up, across the lawns and up the stairs seeking me. What a benediction!

On the transit buses in Cairo, always a stopover, when you travelled from India to Enugu in the sixties, I listened to Arab music, while I waited for everybody's luggage to be found. On one occasion, a young man travelling to the United Kingdom had only carry-on luggage and the airline staff became highly suspicious of him. He kept on saying he had no other luggage, but they wouldn't believe him. Both parties had poor English and communicated badly. So all the other passengers waited for over two hours in the transit bus, which would take us to our hotel. We listened to the piped music and I discovered that the keening sound, unattractive to begin with, was growing on me.

Then there was *Byela* in Colombo in the late fifties, the kind of rhythm, which made your feet dance under the table. In the Eighty club, which at that time, was my sister-in-law's favourite watering hole, the patrons moved sinuously to that Sinhalese sound; since I didn't have anything to contribute to the conversation, having only recently arrived in Colombo, I watched the dancers.

My travels had not been planned. Quite by chance, I was fortunate to end up in just-liberated West Africa, in the tumultuous early sixties, when I was still young enough to learn to dance the Highlife. Even in minuscule towns like *Ikot Ekpene*, a good five-hour journey by road from Enugu, there would be a small shop, which sold everything that Nigerians needed: ghari, salt, piri-piri, Fanta, groundnut oil, cloth... and beer. My husband got his

67

regular supply of fire-water from there. He would go in with his empty beer crate now and then to exchange it for a full one, and I'd sit in the car with my boys waiting for him.

Music would blare loud enough to abolish all thought and I would watch my surroundings zombie-like. A small crowd of children, boys and girls around four to ten years of age, would be loitering outside; as the music started they would begin dancing. The little bodies moved beautifully, short arms and legs flying in all directions and the hips and behinds rotating to the rhythm. That was one dance I was determined to learn.

I got my students at *Ifuho* Teacher Training College to teach me, in exchange for me showing them how to drape a sari. That was some years before the queen visited Accra and danced the Highlife with President Nkrumah; in Nigeria, a destructive civil war had intervened in 1966, and normal life had been suspended for a while.

When I came to live in England several years later, in 1974, after spending five years in Zambia, on the Copper belt, I missed the sounds of Africa; I thought I'd never hear them again. One day, however, quite by chance, I acquired tickets for a show in the West End; a troupe called *Ipi Tombe* was performing, and the drums and the dances took me all the way back to Africa.

I got into the habit of looking for the music of other countries. In Zambia, all along the motorways, the petrol stations would have music from Congo and South Africa in their loud speakers, rather than Highlife. In 1995, travelling from Lusaka to Kasama in the north, on a second spell in Zambia, I would stop to fill up on the way, and the music would draw me in. *Bongoman* was everywhere in the forecourts of petrol stations. There wouldn't be much traffic on those roads at the early hours I travelled, and I would feel free to dance in the forecourt all alone. Sometimes one of the counterparts on our project would join me. 'I didn't know Indian women did this kind of thing,' he said to me once.

I ended up with a smorgasbord of music in my head because of that unusual man who decided he was going to make me into a different kind of *Malayalee* girl.

9

My cousin, Appu -- or Appuettan -- four years older than me, was rather more permanent than most of the family that landed up in our house for a day or two and disappeared. He went away for a few years now and then without notice, like much of the flotsam in that house in Thalassery, but he invariably came back. Even I could see that he was, in some manner, entitled. He was the son of my father's brother, the *pauthran* (son of a son) of my ageing achamma; it was his job to light the pyre when she died. He had cachet even in the other world.

Appuettan was more there in our house than not, and I adored him. I could never figure out why because he ignored me and had no time at all for females in general; they were known to be inferior to all males. But, when he had to memorise poetry, '*A boy stood on the burning deck*,' for his exams, he would recite it to me from the latrine, door left open but out of sight for the duration, and I would have to stand on the back-veranda nearby, and check against the textbook. He was a good student and at exam time, he did not stop studying just to defecate. I was his chattel; I think he would have sent me to defecate for him if he could.

Initially, he attended *Koduvally* School, a few

minutes' walk from my house, just across from the Koduvally river, after which it was named. However, in 1939, my father decided the local school was not good enough for Appuettan. He had to go to the St Joseph's Boys' High School in the centre of town, a mile away. This was an English-medium school, and like all Catholic schools in Kerala, had a reputation for being better than the state schools. Much later in life, when I worked in Nigeria or Zambia or some other African country, I could see the same belief at work – the catholic schools were better. Even more surprisingly, the same belief operates in England – if not a grammar school, then the Catholic Secondary Schools are best.

Achan entrusted his nephew, Madhavan, with the job of taking Appuettan to The Saint Joseph's Secondary school and enrolling him there. I begged to go with them in the *jutka* for a ride into town. Achan, busy with clients, in the corner of our veranda, which he had converted into his office, hardly noticed me getting into the *jutka*. There was a crowd squeezed into the rickety bench on which his clients sat; he was a criminal lawyer and these men were all probably on bail.

When we returned from the trip a few hours later, I was keeping my head down. I had been particularly naughty knowing Madhavettan would not know how to deal with me if I threw a sudden googly. So, after Appuettan had been enrolled and we got into the jutka to return home, I kicked up a huge tantrum saying I wanted to go to school as well. I was then four years old, and strangely, remember this incident vividly. Madhavan was forced to take me to the Sacred Heart Girls' School nearby and enrol me in

71

year one.

When Achan heard Madhavan had enrolled me in the Sacred Heart Girls School without reference to him, he was not amused. My achamma even less. She had not been able to check auspicious moments to begin my schooling; this was her territory. My father called her rituals and omens hocus-pocus, and disapproved actively, so she would pick a moment when he was out of the house to do the exorcising of evil eyes and dangerous diseases. She firmly believed that smallpox came into a house, sent by an evil woman, called *Mariamma*, and the only way to keep the demon at bay was to leave half-shells of empty coconuts on either side of our walkway, filled with a thin solution of cow-dung.

Thus did my schooling begin, a little earlier than necessary, and almost by accident. What didn't become pertinent till eleven years later was the fact that Madhavettan had no idea what my date-of-birth was. So he made a wild guess -- and got it wrong by about two months. What's a month or two in a long life? I, like everyone else in those days, did not have a birth-certificate; it hardly mattered. I have never had one since. The School-Leaving Certificate, which I got in 1950, is accepted all over India as a substitute for a birth certificate.

I found out that my date-of-birth was recorded incorrectly, when my Secondary School Leaving Certificate (SSLC) exams approached. I was fourteen years old. Mother Theckla, the headmistress called each student in our year one by one, into her office. We were shown our certificate books and asked to sign for the accuracy. According to the certificate book, I was born on first March 1935. I knew I was not born in March as my family always said I was born in the Malayalam month of *Medam*, which falls between mid-April and mid-May.

I also knew I was born under the *Bharani* star and all this was recorded in my father's little diary. As Malayalees celebrate the star-day rather than the calendar date, the birthday in each year could fall anywhere between mid-April and mid-May, but not in March. I said all this to Mother Theckla. Not being a Hindu herself, she had no idea as to what I was talking about. She asked me to come back and talk to her the next day.

When I saw her the next day, she insisted I would not be able to sit my exams that year if I was listed as born in May. I had to be fifteen *before* the exam and the exams started in April. Mother Superior suggested I forget about the error, to avoid having to wait another year before taking the exams; I agreed to do so. It seemed of no consequence.

Achamma had been denied her role in the household when I started at school. She had not been able to consult the *Panchangam*, the holy book with the auspicious times and dates. She was disgusted. Her rituals were normally directed towards invoking the blessings of a large pantheon of Hindu gods and warding off evil eyes and spirits. This much-venerated book, the Panchangam, was about the positions of planets and stars in the firmament at any given moment and what configurations would provide the most auspicious time to do anything special.

Achamma's copy was quite old – the Panjangam

prophesied for five years at a time, so it tended to be consulted well beyond its disintegration. It was a thin book with yellowing pages, the tiny print and crammed lines making up for the lack of paper-space. Our copy smelled of old newspaper and incense. The booklet generally rested behind the plaster statue of the blue Krishnan, which was the centrepiece of our indoor shrine in the *padingitta (central room)*.

That shrine was also the centre-piece of our life. When we children came in from play in the evenings, and washed, we had to sit in front of the shrine and recite our prayers and incantations. *'Ramaramarama'* fifty times was one of them. We did it at break-neck speed, Appuettan, Mani and I lined up in front of the lighted nilavilakku. Another was a hymn to Saraswathy, the goddess of education and prosperity. We were not fed till after we'd said our prayers and put sacred ash on our foreheads. The ash, gritty to the touch, was kept near the Krishnan-image in a brass tray, which always had a few burnt-out matchsticks in it. The place smelled of gingelly oil, ash and sandalwood.

Crepe paper in many colours and shiny gold and silver paper cut into moon and star shapes, as well as calendar pictures of Saraswathy, Shivan, Krishnan, and all Achamma's Gods (and there were many) decorated the prayer corner. Here the nilavilakku, the sacred lamp, was lighted at dawn and dusk. That familiar smell of sulphur, oil and ash would mean the beginning of another day. During the scarcities of the war years, it would be just one valiant wick instead of the customary five in more prosperous times

If I behaved myself, Ammamma would let me help cut the crepe paper, but I knew I wasn't good at it. For us, at that time, a few sheets of card or coloured paper was a huge luxury. These days, I look at my granddaughter's store of stationery: cards of many hues, colour pencils by the dozens, even some for the dog to chew, markers, stickers, glue of different kinds (we used rice-paste), and I think – all this and i-phones too. Not to mention sleep-overs, days spent in the houses of friends, and trips to shopping malls. The nature of school-life has changed. I think the nature of grandmother-hood has also changed. My perspective is troglodyte.

I remember begging over-cooked rice from the kitchen and mashing it with my fingers into paste; the nuns at school used flour. If we needed foolscap paper for homework, Ammamma would give us a quarter-anna for one precious sheet. As for colour pencils, I remember one, half blue, half red, so that the two ends were two different colours.

And sleepovers? Nice Malayalee girls were not allowed to spend nights at some other family's home. What if the father was a drunk? Or beat up his wife in front of the children? The question of shopping malls did not arise because the concept of shopping as a leisure activity did not exist.

We didn't have pocket money either. You only bought things that you needed, and in the days of plastic-free existence, apart from textiles (no ready-made garments then) and minimal beauty products, what was there to buy? I remember Cuticura powder, which was our sole aid to beauty, and the *pottu (decorative dot on the forehead)* and *kohl(eyeliner)*. D-I-Y *Chandu* (thick coloured liquid) for the pottu was made from rice flour, and kohl was created from a clean rag dipped in lime juice and burnt on to a piece of clay. The soot was scraped off and mixed with gingelly oil to form a hard paste. We depended on the flowers in our hair, long before Aung San Suu Kyi, to make us sparkle.

When Achamma heard that I had started school without the benefit of her selection of auspicious days and times, she hawked and spat red betel juice in frustration. But she didn't dare raise it with my father; she knew he would have no sympathy for her. Achamma muttered and murmured her displeasure for a whole day and took to her bed as a protest. Achan did not notice, but Ammamma reminded her gently that Achan did not believe in the *Panjangam* and wouldn't notice her sulks anyway. When my father was ill with bronchitis, as he often was, she would stand on the bottom steps of the staircase to his bedroom and do the casting away of evil spirits and envious eyes. It had nothing to do with his smoking according to her. Of course.

Did my achamma know of the diverse paths my religious education took under the nuns at Sacred Heart? If she did, she would have been horrified. For prayers, we were taught *Hail Marys* and the *Lord's Prayer*. Most Wednesdays we were led around the *Ways of the Cross* in the beautiful little chapel in the school-yard. There was Angelus twice a day, when the special bells would ring out alerting us. Then there was the *Act of Contrition*. If you failed to say it before you went to sleep, the devil would get your soul. And if you died in your sleep, the hell-fires awaited you.

Limbo was the destination of the unfortunate infant who died without informing the church of his existence and getting baptised. What a God! And, in Limbo, there was no remission for good behaviour – you stayed there to eternity. All of us had one slim chance, in spite of our sins, mortal and venial, after a long and unpredictable wait; there would be a *second coming* and we could be forgiven and bypass purgatory, to go straight to heaven. Sisters defined moral and venial sins to us in great detail so that we understood some sins were more vile than others.

Sister painted graphic pictures of the devil, with flaming torso, waiting to engulf all the feckless Hindu girls who went home and changed faith, back to Ramaramarama and the many depraved Gods of the Hindu pantheon every day. I was comfortable oscillating between the two religions, and today, I find that that early accommodation to any religion that comes by, sustains my sense of the ludicrous regarding all of them.

Then there were the Jesus-pictures, which we were encouraged to collect. Like collecting match-labels. The nuns must have made a decent profit there.

Our first lesson every morning was Moral Science. It began with Catechism:
"Who made you?
God made me.
Why did God make you?
To love him, to obey him…"
Sounded like a training scheme for Kerala wives.

The locals called our school the Convent and it was that as well. Tucked away on a side-road, near the centre of town, the market and the bus-stand, but aloof from the life of the town, the Sacred Heart Girls' was spread wide on one side of that unnamed road. As buildings went in Thalassery at that time, it was an imposing building, with separate wings for the first years and infant classes. The number of students increased over the years after Independence and the school spread, filling up the empty ground between chapel and classrooms. I wonder whether the mango tree at which I used to throw stones during the lunch hour has been sacrificed for stone and mortar.

Opposite the school and slightly to the left was the Victoria library, where I cultivated an addiction to the smell of old books. Saint Joseph's Boys', the Catholic school for boys, was just a minute's walk away. A small flock of nuns lived in the convent; they rarely ventured outside the premises, except when they attended mass at the Saint Joseph's chapel across the road.

The irreverent among the Thalassery men (and the town's default position was irreverent) called them '*Krishnapparanthu*' a common brown-and-white hawk, after the colours of their ankle-length brown habits, with the white wimple, that the Sisters wore. The long habits were made of serge and they wore a thick leather belt to keep it together. From the side of the belt, a knee-length rosary dangled; a cross hung on a silver chain round the neck. The neck itself was covered with wimple and of course the head also was covered. They wore thick shoes. In the weather of Thalassery, this costume must have been as self-flagellation is to Shia Muslims. Penance!

The town's mockery of the nuns was partly due to

78

frustration as the nuns did not speak Malayalam; they were from Mangalapuram eighty miles away, and their language was *Konkini*. So, as far as Thalassery was concerned, they were aliens. On the very rare occasions the nuns went past our houses, Mani, my cousin, and I, would run to the gate to stare at them. They always walked abreast of each other in a solid line, sublimely ignoring the traffic on the narrow roads. In Malayalam they were called *Kanyasthree*, virgin maidens, and the buses hurtling down Court Road slowed down for them. For all the levity of the men around, the nuns were treated with grudging respect.

The Sacred Hear Girls' High School and the Saint Joseph's Boys' High School were the two schools of choice for the aspiring middle-classes in the 1930s and onwards in Thalassery. The teachers were mostly nuns in the Girls' school and priests in the Boys' school. They shared the one Catholic Chapel in town, and sometimes the priests from over the road, came to the convent to take a Sunday service, in their small chapel, or pray for a special cause. When they came by, it was interesting to see that the nuns treated the priests with the kind of deference that women in our households generally reserved for their husbands and other alpha-males in the family.

We had a few lay teachers; some of them boarded in a line of rooms, at the back of the chapel attached to the school. I did not, as a child in the years just after the war, realise, how poor the establishment in the convent was. The nuns constantly invented events to raise money – they needed more classrooms with the sudden burgeoning of girls' education after independence, in 1947. So we had lucky dips and collection forays, lotteries and festivals, and in the end several classrooms were built. The parents were relieved when the whole building programme was completed and they did not have to respond to urgent demands for money. The nuns could make it quite unpleasant for the children, whose parents refused to part with the tithe. The money in this case was generally four annas or eight annas (half a rupee) for the dips and entertainment. But most households, certainly ours, did not have the change to spare.

The nuns were a canny lot who always knew which family was a soft touch; from those families they demanded five rupees. So many of us had to beg and plead for our guardians to part with that precious five rupees.

Our school did not have adequate playing fields – for netball we had to go to the Collector's compound. This was the grandest mansion in Thalassery, where the most important civil-servant, the Sub-Collector, our demi-God, lived, on top of the hill, just above Saint Joseph's Boys' School. Before Independence in 1947, it had always been British men who stayed in this house, and literally, 'collected,' all the numerous taxes extracted from every place and person in India, by the Empire.

The few Indians, who had gone to the United Kingdom, and sat the Indian Civil Service exams, (ICS), and passed, became Collectors too, Deputy Gods in their domains, not more than a handful each year to begin with. These old, dignified mansions where the Collectors lived could always be found in any former British colony, on top of the hill and facing the sea or river. So much so, that decades later, when I went searching for the residence of the Chief Administrative Officer in Magburuka in Sierra Leone, with my colleague, Paul, from the British Council, I could effortlessly guide him in the direction of the hill.

The boys' school, which nestled below a wooded hill, was an adjunct to the church, practically overhanging the Arabian sea. The famous Thalassery Fort, looked down upon it, from its impressive height of ten-metres, with the lighthouse at one end. From here Cardamom, timber, hill products and natural spices were exported all over the world.

The French came first in the seventeenth century, establishing trading posts in Mahe, four miles south of Thalassery, and later Pudussery, on the east coast. As usual the British followed and established a factory north of Thalassery. There was strong opposition to the colonial activities from most of the chieftains on the Malabar coast, but some supported the British. The fort was built by the British to withstand the attacking local chiefs, and subsequently the French.

As French activity increased and opposition to British presence in the region became more evident, the British strengthened the fort to safeguard its interests. They also took possession of Dharmadam island, a mile from my home. The British retained a strong military presence on the Malabar coast from 1776 to 1784. In recent years the head-quarters of the Kottayam district, in which Thalassery is situated, has moved to Cunnoor, about fourteen miles north of Thalassery. The fort itself has been declared a heritage site and is a well-known tourist attraction.

The first ever cricket tournament, of Europeans against locals, was played in the Thalassery maidanam, which the Fort overlooks, and there is a strong tradition of cricket in Thalassery dating from that time – something that was bequeathed by the British.

First the Moghul emperor, Hyder Ali, and later Tippu Sultan, tried to gain control in Malabar but were defeated and had to cede Malabar to the British in the late eighteenth century. In my childhood, my father and I would walk up to the ramparts of the fort to look at the old gun emplacements, facing out to the sea. Below was our *Big maidanam*, a large tract of grass-land, where Thalassery folk took the breeze in the evenings, barefooted boys and men played football, and the goats and cows grazed in the day, around the huge, old *Aalmaram* (Bo tree) in one corner, with centuries-old lianas reaching for the ground. A circular parapet had been built around it to accommodate the town's beggars, layabouts and those waiting for news or action from the Magistrate's Court diagonally opposite. You will find the Cosmopolitan Club, the local watering hole opposite the Magistrate's Court, where the town's middle-classes congregate daily to nurture their sick livers, which some wags say can be found littering the roads surrounding the club. In the early forties, it was a place for seeing bioscopes – silent films in the time of Charlie Chaplin.

The Indian Civil Service, since independence, is known as the IAS, the Indian Administrative Service, and exams are conducted in Delhi. In the days of the Empire, exams were conducted in

England and any Indian who tried to get in had to be, not only academically gifted, but also have the wherewithal to travel to England, be city-bred and fluent in English (they went together), and as British as possible in outlook, attitude and life-style. Also, there should be not the slightest whiff of rebellion against the British Raj and the status quo. Today the Collectors (still the same name!) are selected from common or -garden Indians who have passed the punishing selection exams.

My school, The Sacred Heart Girls High School was just around the corner from the club and the maidanam. Those of us girls (girls?) who are still compos-mentis, aged between sixty years and above, talk with nostalgia about the school we went to, where we learned to tread that strange and difficult cusp between girl and woman. We are functional in the English language because the Sisters fined any girl who spoke anything but English on the premises, a quarter-anna. And quarter-anna was a handful of gooseberries in front of the school-gates; an A4 card in your favourite colour to draw on, or a few orange-sweets at Usman's shop near my home, which displayed an array of multi-coloured penny-sweets in tall glass jars in front.

Things changed drastically in 1947, with Independence. English lost its place in the hierarchy of class-room subjects; it became just an extra language. Teachers had to teach all subjects, overnight, in local languages, in our case, Malayalam. Now, someone had to write Mathematics books and Geography books and all other books in Malayalam.

I was lucky – my father had insisted that I read as many Malayalam books as English. Our teachers, however, had to undergo a sudden realignment. Sister Cordelia, our class teacher, did not speak Malayalam. She taught us British History – our History syllabus had a large tract of British History and not much Indian History. How was she going to manage explaining the Reformation in Malayalam without any spoken Malayalam in her head?

The lay teachers now came into their own. Bred to the culture of the Convent, even *their* facility in Malayalam was suspect. I remember Hazel teacher teaching my class about parallel lines. She tripped around, speaking mostly in English, then painfully translating. She was probably one of our most efficient teachers, but the technical words in Malayalam defeated her. She still continued with right angles and congruent triangles, having no other name for them. A year later the Malayalam Maths books arrived and she learned to say *samanthara rekhagal*; parallel lines had undergone a sea-change.

Amazingly, over the years, when I returned to India from many godforsaken places and posts, I found my language had left me behind. It had come far to meet the demands of the twentieth century and the space age, and there now seemed nothing that could not be said in Malayalam.

The nuns ignored the world around them and made their own rules. For instance, all other schools closed every weekend, Saturdays and Sundays. The Sacred Heart closed on Thursdays and Sundays, and to this day I have not found out why. They also insisted that we kept a spare set of clothes (no uniforms in those days) to change into, if we got wet walking to school. For us, girls, the whole point of a rainy day was to get really drenched so that the nuns would be forced to send us home. Bliss! A whole school-day off to do more important things – pick mangoes, play *Thalama* -- other than sit in a classroom. So, we conveniently 'forgot' to bring the non-existent spare set in. In any case, I can't remember having spare clothes; what I remember is my cousin, Naani, hanging our school-clothes over the fireplace, during the rainy season, to make it dry quicker. The clothes always smelled of wood-smoke and the rice-starch used in the washing, to give it a semblance of life.

We had our year-ending exams in early April and schools closed mid-April to avoid the searing heat of May. We generally went back to school in the first week of June. During May, if we were lucky we would have got our clothes for the new year. Mani and I got two frocks each – hence the strategies to dry them.

Many of us in the school managed with scant provision for school. The only girls who came in wearing satin and silks, ringing the changes and showing off, were the ones with brothers working in East Africa. These brothers came back once in four or five years, from Zanzibar and Kampala, Nairobi and Kisumu, loaded with rich silks and georgettes for their families. They would come to find a bride if they were still single and go back with their new, just-unpacked partners for another five years.

Today some of the men who go to the Gulf states to make money, come back after two to three years. Their first obligation is to provide dowries for their sisters and tile the thatched roof of their houses.

Then they could get married, leave their wives behind and go away for some years. The gulf states do not allow the wives of blue collar workers to accompany them.

And yet, though Mani and I didn't have rich clothes, I did not have a sense of deprivation – our household considered clothes as an essential for going out, no more than that. The girls who were well-turned out looked down on us, but the majority were like us.

Shopping had no entertainment value. If there was excess money, it went to the poor wing of the extended family for school-fees, clothes... We were well-loved and that was all that mattered.

10

Soon after he returned from his studies in Madanapalle, my father had set up practice at the District Courts, only a hop-skip-and-a-jump from our home, which he rented for a few months. That was where I was born. He pointed it out to me on one of our morning walks down that way. He moved to another house around the corner, about five minutes' walk away sometime in 1936; indeed all the newly graduated lawyers rented homes there because the Civil Courts were so near. So, gradually, it became Court Road, and people started addressing letters in that name.

To begin with, there were just three or four lawyers, education even for men was not a serious proposition so long as there was land to live off. Most families managed with the produce from their compounds. There were coconuts, plantain, bananas, yams, jack fruit and mangoes in most gardens in the countryside. If you also farmed some rice, you were reasonably well-provided for. The men, sometimes, did odd jobs as messengers for the offices in town, in between looking after their land.

One of my father's sisters lived in this manner; she didn't need much cash. I remember that when I went for a holiday to her house, I would join her sons in watering the vegetables that had been planted in her fields when the harvest was in. There would be hillocks of rice on her veranda and her forecourt; as they dried the rice would be boiled, husked and put away. There was an aura of prosperity in that household though she would not have even five rupees in her pan box.

Going to college was a new venture and few thought about it. When my father graduated, he was one of the first of three young men from his village to complete a degree course. The nearest college which offered a degree course was in far-away Madras (now Chennai) and involved both expense and inconvenience. Between ten and eleven in the morning I could count off the black-coated and gowned young men walking the short distance to the Courts, followed by their touts carrying papers, folded length-wise into leather folders, and clients at a respectful distance behind. In my childhood I remember four of them, all young men, newly married, with children in Primary School. No female lawyers then, or indeed female much else, and the first female lawyer did not join the Thalassery Bar till the seventies.

That house on Court Road was to all intents and purposes the home I grew up in; anything that came after, wherever in the world they were, were way-stations.

Until age and distemper caught up with me, I did an annual pilgrimage to Thalassery; I always returned to England feeling replenished in spirit, wondering how long that feeling would last. When I am in that little, Government-forsaken, back-water of a town, even my grey cells stir and gear up for action.

I feel more Indian – I wear saris more often and

take out my Indian jewellery, and the *pottu* box comes out from the recesses of the dressing table. My eyes get a lining of *kohl*, which will seep into the wrinkles below and proclaim my age. It doesn't last long; the cotton saris that I favour need to be starched and dried, the weather is unfriendly and an overcoat above the sari is an abomination. The *Kohl* and *Pottu* don't do much for my ravaged face either.

Looking at my valiant, but half-dead almond tree in my bleak, front garden here in Purley in winter and remembering the lush green of my home-country, I think of this journey, this annual pilgrimage with wonder. If I travel by car I see the countryside getting gradually more devoid of development as we leave South Malabar behind.

There is a jinx on North Malabar, specially Thalassery and its little satellite villages -- with good reason too. This part of Kerala is notorious for its violent politics and for the political assassinations, which are commonplace. In October 1995, a group of Naxalites went into a Primary classroom, in a small village called Mokeri, not far from my father's birthplace, armed with machetes. They attacked the class-teacher who belonged to the *Bharathiya Janatha Party*, (which is the ruling party at the Centre since 2016) as the terrified children watched. Blood splattered on to desks, wall and table, and the shirts of children in the front row. Dipping fingers in blood, the killers wrote on the blackboard, 'The same thing will happen to whoever tells on us.'

Naxalite violence was not unusual in Kerala, or indeed in some other parts of India, but this, in front of children, was a horrific first. The *Naxalite* movement (a Maoist movement) had started in the

Naxalbhari village in West Bengal, killing many rich farmers and policemen, as retaliation for the injustices inflicted on the poor by the greedy landowners and the police-arm of the state. Kerala, always a Communist state since the early fifties, quickly copied the terrible bloodletting in Bengal.

Those Naxalites made my part of the world renowned for political assassinations, and the state Government in Thiruvananthapuram struck us off their responsibility-roll, like a badly-behaved secondary student, beyond redemption. Even the undiscriminating *Janashathabdi* train from Kochi to the North refuses to go beyond Kozhikode; it stops about sixty-five kilometres south of Thalassery. We have to travel from Kochi, where I had made a home in 1999, on the dilapidated *Eranad*, which stops at every telegraph pole with a crow on it; it still had squatting toilets, old seats and dirt-filled dining trays to cater for us -- or we could change trains.

However- and this is a big however-- as the train draws into Mahe, that tiny enclave of French territory of the past, about six kilometres from Thalassery, I know already that I'm almost home. I talk with absolute confidence to all the people at the door getting off at Mahe. Indeed there is a small group in front of the door, introducing themselves and spreading goodwill. The young man and wife, getting off here, have to practically jump off, children and luggage in hand, because the train stops at Mahe only for a breath-and-a-half. All of us help them to disembark.

The last time I travelled that way, a Muslim couple told me that they were returning from Dubai after two years; that explained the many suitcases. They had a lot to unload in a very short time, so they got down with the children first and we passed the suitcases to them. A young man invited me to his *Niramala* offering at the *Thiruvangad* temple, when the image of God would be festooned with garlands of fresh flowers in his name.

My maternal grandmother lived near the temple and she never missed a Niramala. When I was visiting she would take me along; I have a memory of bells, *chenda* (Kerala drums) and cymbals, smell of wicks burning in the huge Nilavilakkus in hot coconut oil, jasmine and sandalwood. And the ever-present sandalwood paste. When the puja was finished the pujari would give every devotee *kalabam* (sandalwood paste) and holy *Thulasi* leaf, and the men and women would touch the blessed kalabam to their foreheads. On the oily steps, the crowd always pushed and thrust out with shoulders to be in front, and it was a bit of an obstacle course.

Talking to the people around you is de rigueur here in this old part of North Malabar, no vacant stares past your face as I get elsewhere in Kerala, certainly not the cool summing up I receive on the Tube in London. Well, I've all that in front of me in another three weeks, I always think. So there, on my all-too-brief visits, I generally stocked up on human warmth and the sheer joy of belonging.

I know now that I will never belong anywhere but in that little coastal town, which is rediscovering itself. The cosmetic surgery, with grey concrete and chrome is unbecoming, but only bits are gone. Most of Thalassery is blessedly old, a little shabby and natural. I shouldn't complain; in my childhood, there

91

was one government hospital in town; it was near the beach and as you walked past, you could see the sick men and women, too poor to afford private doctors, sprawled on benches and the floor, waiting to be seen. Not unlike the A and E at NHS hospitals recently

Now there are two huge hospitals in Thalassery, one near my grandfather's old village, Moozhikkara. It is ugly, its front gate crowded into a busy road, all concrete and glass, but it serves its purpose. Sick men and women do not have to travel five miles to reach a hospital in an emergency. Similarly, there is another huge hospital on the road where I lived my childhood and adolescent years.

There is a stadium where the paddy fields used to stretch peaceably as far as eye could see; now cricket rules, O K. The Koduvally river has shrunk into itself. A river that gave name to and defined that whole area has morphed into apologetic little rivulets. I cannot find my way around my hometown.

On these visits, I always go to my old house, (which my father built in 1950, the year I joined the local college,) to chat to my dead father, can we ever quite see him off? He lingers. I normally pick up a few grains of mud from the spot where he was cremated and drop them into my purse. The money-plastic will be gritty for a few weeks and the holes-in-the-wall in England may find another reason to refuse me my hard-earned dosh. Ah well –

My father always maintained that when he died there should not be any religious rituals attached to his cremation.

'The beach near our house is where I should end,' he used to say, but when he died in Kozhikode, his nephew had little control over the day. A deputation from Thalassery claimed his body saying, 'He belongs to Thalassery.' They came with a van and took him back home.

There was no stopping them; they organised a public meeting with loud speakers and the whole town seemed to have turned up to see him off. Men lined the road when the compound was full; his man-Friday told me that many were in tears.

I can hear his amused aside. 'They have nothing better to do.'

The last time I went I could not reach the spot where he was cremated, as the compound is grown over, the undergrowth is a few feet high and dense. There were snakes there always (sometimes they ventured into the house and the cats taunted them) and I didn't go close. Instead I said in my mind to my father: *I shall not come this way again. You are gone by now. You would not abide this desecration.*

The stadium is now complete in the fields where I roamed, where the young men battened the ground down and played badminton after the harvest, fished for river-fish in the shallow waters of the paddy-fields and I gazed between turning the pages of my latest book. There is nothing to look at now. The house has been 'acquired' and is slowly dwindling away before the offices of the stadium are built there.

The cast-iron gate, which was my father's pride and joy, has broken down and someone has carted it off. The concrete slabs at the entrance are breaking up.

The house itself is dismal. Male nurses from the nearby Co-operative Hospital are lodging there and doing to the house what young men do when they have no resources and no style. Colourful *lungis* (sarongs) and greying underpants hang on a rope on the balcony, to dry. The woodwork is rotting, the front office window is hanging on one hinge, and the young man walking on the terrace upstairs seems part of that dilapidation.

I am glad to get away to my cousin's house, where I am staying for the night, and the welcome of my family. Forget the tasteless mall, the dried-up river bed and all else that we call modernisation.

I know I'll keep going back to that road, that place, in spite of the shambles it has become -- will the remnants see me out too? Last through the fag end of my life? I hope so.

11

In 1940, my world in Thalassery changed. Appuettan, my father's beloved elder brother's son, came back from Penang after spending some months with his parents, but this time his sister, Mani, who was only six months older than me, came with him for schooling to India. War-clouds were gathering in Malaysia now and Velyachan (Achan's elder brother) had to get his children away quickly. Velyachan worked on the rubber estates in Penang at that time, and the only schools around were the inadequate schools the estate owners provided for the labourers. Indeed my Velyachan was a doctor and spent his professional life delivering babies of the estate women. So much so that when he returned home and set up a private practice in Ottappalam, where his wife's family lived, he refused to look at another vagina.

I now had a constant companion and she remains, to this day, the closest family member that I have in India. Caring, exasperating, demanding and loyal, she knows more about me than anyone else in the world. My father had a special soft spot for her; if we wanted a special concession from him, like permission to go to the cinema, or five rupees for sugar for a *payasam*, we sent her to do the asking.

Appuettan, her brother, however, thought all

womankind inferior to his male existence and had little to do with us girls. He was naughty, throwing stones at windows, annoying the shop-owner, Mammadu, who had a tiny veranda-shop, two metres from our front-gate. This had serious consequences when Appuettan tried to perfect his bowling action every weekend, on the walkway to our front-gate. The ball often swung and hit Mammadu's pile of dry coconut shells, which he sold for using in the coal iron, for ironing clothes. The stone generally toppled his careful pyramid of shells and Mammadu would go ballistic. When Appuettan had chalked up enough misdemeanours, Mammadu would accost Achan at the gate with his loud complaints, periodically hawking and spitting red beteljuice in frustration.

Achan hated this kind of encounter; Mammadu would always find him as he returned from the Courts in the evening, tired and ill-tempered. Appuettan would be summoned and cross-examined in legal detail. Did he? When? Why? It always ended in Appuettan being caned. Afterwards, Appuettan would have tears running down his cheeks; Achan would be miserable because he hated what he had done, and us girls would slink around with a sense of catastrophe. We hated Mammadu -- until he sent us fresh bananas the next day as a peace offering.

Achan had this theory that girls should not be caned, but boys needed it to make them well-behaved young men. In fact most people in authority caned both girls and boys. In the Sacred Heart High School where I spent eleven years the Headmistress had no qualms – she caned the girls in public, in front of morning assembly, though caning was rare. I never found out what the transgressions were.

Mani and I had pastimes, like spying on our half-naked neighbour, which would probably have got us the cane from Sister Felix. In mitigation, we did not have too many ready-made pastimes then – no Snakes-and-Ladders, no Ludo; the situation led to inventiveness.

We collected the fallen leaves of the Jackfruit trees, folded them and pinned them with the spine of palm fronds, and pretended we were selling cattle in the market. We bargained, got angry and became poor or rich in cattle-money. This was our version of Monopoly.

We collected small, glossy stones and played *chottu-kali* and *Kottam-kallu*. The seeds that fell off the arecanut tree were our source for *chottu*, which involved, throwing a handful on the flat surface of the cement floor on the veranda, and using a master-seed, flicking at the rest one by one, without touching more than one at any time. *Kotham kallu* was played with stones, throwing one up and sweeping as many up as you could with your fist as the one thrown up came down. You had to be quick and skilful.

Then there was *Thalama*. For this we made a small ball by plaiting coconut leaf-fronds around a stone. You would end up with a cube aspiring to be a circle. We had many games, throwing and catching and batting this ball with a bat, again made from the thick middle-spine of the coconut palm leaf. There was no part of the coconut tree, which was not useful; even the trunk was used in buildings.

When we had a lot of time to kill, we wandered over to the house behind us. We called it *Echiveedu*,

97

(sisters' house) because the two sisters living there were single and indulged us with delicacies and allowed us to pick mangoes and wind-fall tamarind from their compound. It was a huge and sprawling, the likes of which no longer exist in Thalassery, where the land has been cut up into smaller and even smaller pieces to build Dubai, Qatar, Saudi Arabia or Bahrain-funded houses.

The sisters also kept goats and chickens, which my father would not allow in our house, saying they brought mosquitos. Next door we were allowed to see the mother-hens sitting patiently over their eggs and the new-born kids trying to haul themselves on to their feet. There can't be many more enthralling sights to a child than that of the mother-goat indulgently watching her brood gambol around her. Sadly, the butcher would come at some time and lead some of the kids away, and the mother would grieve and bay for many days after. The sisters would cry too, but this was a livelihood and they had no choice. I could hear the mother-goat calling out to her brood in the dead of the night for a day or two; it made me pull the blanket over my head to shut that agony out.

For us girls the life-style in *Echiveedu* was a lesson in self-sufficiency, which could not be practised in our home, even if we had the skill, which we didn't, because we had very little land attached to our building. Echiveedu was a modest little house, in the middle of a terraced compound, full of coconut trees, mango trees and Jack trees. In one section a huge Tamarind tree spread its shade wide, and around it, many indigenous trees flourished. I remember a coffee bush from which one of the sisters would collect coffee pods for their morning drink. She would roast the pods in a dry wok and pound it in a mortar with a wooden pestle, until it became recognisable coffee powder.

The coconut trees provided not only coconuts to use in cooking, but also palm leaf for the thatch and trunks to use on chicken coops and goat sheds. The roof got thatched every other year and all the thatch was made in the house by hand.

The palm leaves were soaked for many days to soften, then split down the middle. Then the two sisters would plait them in a large basket weave. After that they would be dried for a while and put away in the outhouse. The thatching itself was done by men and for that, all the able-bodied men in the neighbourhood would assemble early in the morning of the thatching day. The women would cook conjee and fish and cassava for them. Mani and I would run around enjoying the bustle and watching the men take down the old thatch in preparation for putting up the new.

The women would carefully separate the good, serviceable thatch, which could be used again, from the rest, which would become fuel for the house. The whole house would be finished in a day.

The fruit from the Tamarind tree would also be seeded once a year and stocked in tall earthenware jars, for use in the kitchen. They made their soap from the fruit of the *Cheenikka*; when boiled it came up as a frothy substance, which dried into small misshapen cakes of soap.

Firewood came from the compound and the shells and husks of coconuts were used for the same purpose. The only things they bought were rice, kerosene, cooking oil, fish and, occasionally vegetables. When we went to their house we loved watching the sisters at work, tending goats and chickens. Sometimes they made us an omelette. Theirs was a way of life that has disappeared now – with television, and their classic serials, women don't want to spend too much time making things that they can buy. This is possible because the cash economy has grown and there is money coming in from the jobs of men and women. The gulf states have also put money into the hands of working classes in Kerala.

In the 1940s, only one man in Echiveedu had a regular job; the others found ways of making money in enterprising ways, one by sewing clothes and a second by keeping a small corner shop.

On the left of our house, lived Chaathu, who was a whole institution in himself. A source of endless prurience and entertainment not to mention snippets of Malayalam language that we never came across in our house. He worked nights as a watchman in the European Club, on top of the local *Pallikunnu* hill. He was always wide awake and aggressive in the mornings, then would wind down, just before he went off to sleep for the day. He would sit on his dilapidated armchair on the narrow veranda of his house, only three metres from our kitchen. On bad days you could hear him muttering and building up to an outburst. We were prohibited from going to that side of the house when he was rampant.

He was well-hated in the neighbourhood for his drunken abuse of his wife, Maathu, who was our outside maid. He terrorised his children too, chasing them in alcohol driven frenzies. He could never catch them as they ran faster than him and hid behind the house, in the gully. There was a small *drumstick* tree in the back of the compound and they could get down to the gully by sliding down it.

Chaathu was a watchman at the European club and it was rumoured that he had access to the liquor in the club. It was also rumoured that it was his job to find womankind for the British men who came for R and R. Indians were not allowed on the club compound or premises; indeed there was a sign at the entrance saying so.

However, my father did take me inside these sanctified premises, soon after Independence. A visiting Scottish judge had invited him for tea; I remember the judge seemed surprised that I could speak a little English. He showed me how to play bowls in their indoor bowling alley.

Though Mani and I were strictly forbidden from hanging around on the north side of our house where Chaathu lived in uncomfortable proximity, it was a command difficult to enforce because this end of the house and the narrow, chipped parapet there, were the places where all of us, women and children, did our communal teeth-cleaning, with burnt paddy-husk. The spines of coconut fronds for cleaning tongues were kept in an old Horlicks jar on a window-sill there. When Mani and I arrived there some mornings, Chaathu would already be ensconced on the narrow strip of his veranda, revving up for a proper, verbal assault on the neighbourhood, starting with his silent wife, Maathu.

'*Nayinede mole, Koothicheende mole*,' is how he addressed his wife. 'Daughter of a bitch, daughter of a whore.' Maathu would make a quick exit to the back of the house; she was so acclimatised to his violence that she had stopped being afraid.

Sundays were special: it was Chaathu's day off. His oil-bath day. He would be naked except for a foot-wide piece of frayed, old sacking round his loins. Since he suffered from a massive, pendulous hydrocele, the sacking didn't do much. Mani and I would stare at the objects, especially when he lifted the sacking to oil his crotch. If he caught us staring and giggling, we would run inside, followed by his loud curses. On Sundays, Mani and I had time to do our neighbourhood watch.

In the shop to the left of our house, on the roadside, was a little café. The owner bred beautiful cats and he would give us one now and then. When I was thirteen he brought four all-white fluffy kittens to our house. If he couldn't find homes for the litter, he would put them in a sack and drown them. I wanted the lot, all four of them, but Ammamma allowed only the one. I called her *Sundari* – meaning beauty in Malayalam – because she was absolutely lovely: fluffy white fur, a tail like a feather duster, and an innocent look.

My father disapproved – he believed cats brought asthma. So he didn't like my holding her close or keeping her in my lap for too long. But the two of us, the kitten and I, had our own strategies to avoid his ire; Sundari just jumped down from my lap and sloped off when she heard his footsteps. If he came upon us suddenly, I would hide her in my lap, under my blouse or sari; sometimes she gave the game away by purring loudly.

My family have ever since been animal people – ready to go to great lengths to look after animals. We have always had arrogant cats and irrepressible dogs around us.

Mani and I had strict instructions about where we could or could not wander – *Echiveedu* was alright, but the two houses on the left and right of us were forbidden territory. The extended family on the right had a large brood of children, about my age, running around. Between our compound and theirs was a well and Achan declared it dangerous.

Mani and I were curious about the children next door. When the young mothers in that house got frustrated they beat their children mercilessly. And if they were really naughty, one of them would put ground chilli in the culprit's eyes. This was torture and we hated the mother for it. Not that it stopped any of the children from doing whatever they wanted.

On the other side was Maathu's house. This was also a large extended family, most of the men and women doing the little jobs that keep the wealthy in comfort. They ran small businesses of varying fortunes, so they just about managed. Achan tried to persuade the children to go to school, but they soon dropped out. We were not allowed to go there either because their hearth was at ground level and he was scared we would get burned. Also because of Chaathu, the local terror.

Mani and I largely obeyed Achan when he was around, but when he was out of the house, we could jump from our back garden to Chaathu's veranda without touching ground. And we did. We went to Maathu's house to find her daughter, Leela, who was our age and a friend.

Leela was fair like a *madamma*, just as her mother was. Her long curly hair never got washed unless the sisters from Echiveedu washed it when she visited there. Those sisters indulged all of us girls, though they had none of their own. Leela had stopped going to school after three years and could barely read or write. She never tried to do either. Many years later, I heard she had married a wealthy man who had been bowled over by her unusual looks.

Leela had a different kind of childhood from ours; she was also more mature and self-possessed. Her little hut was eerie; if you stood on the narrow veranda and looked inside, all you could see was darkness. So I would stand outside and call her loudly. If she answered me back, I would know where to find her. Mostly, she was in the kitchen at the back. I would steel myself to walk through that corridor of darkness to find her.

In that fireplace Leela usually burned dry leaves, which her mother had swept up from the many houses where she worked. Her fireplace was just three stones on the floor; I would often find her roasting cassava on the embers in the fireplace. Cassava is the poor man's staple in Kerala, and if you ate it often you would cultivate a taste for it. During the war we had all been forced to eat Cassava and I loved it especially when it was roasted. My father ate it almost daily, pounded into a mash with curried sardines. It was called *puzhukku* and is a staple of Malayalee suppers.

Mani and I were not allowed to go near the fireplace in our house, but none of these rules applied to Leela. When we joined her, she would roast an extra piece of cassava for us. When the skin became burnt, she would prod it out with a stick and we would beat it with the heel of our hands. The skin would part and we could get the delicious farinose flesh out.

When she was small, Leela had followed Maathu around to our house when she came to sweep in the mornings, but she stopped coming after a while. Occasionally I played *kottamkallu* with her, but if any of the adults approached, she would run away.

In addition to Leela I had another friend from across the gully where there was a huge, ancient Muslim house; Aliyumma as about our age too; she lived in that house within a huge extended family, and we would talk across the gully to her. By about eleven years of age, Aliyumma stopped going to school. She began wearing a *thattom*, a short head scarf that was tucked round her head and behind her ears. It was a token gesture unlike the *hijab* of the present day. Made of thin, almost see-through material, it was a minor concession to being a *Mapla* (Kerala Muslim) girl. Indeed the Muslims in Kerala took their *Muslimhood* lightly. Ammamma had a theory that many of them were Hindus forcibly converted during the Mapla rebellions of the nineteen twenties. Aliyumma was beautiful by any standards but seemed totally unaware of this.

Ammamma had distant memories of the Mapla riots of 1921 when hundreds of Hindus and Maplas got killed. She used to insist that there were many forced conversions of Hindus at that time and some of the Maplas of our time were old Hindus. In the twenties the Maplas rioted several times against the Hindu landowners who treated them unjustly. The riots of

1921 were the worst. Sometimes the Hindus and Maplas rioted against the British, the common enemy. In all cases it ended up in huge numbers of Muslims, and a few venturesome Hindus, gunned down, imprisoned, or exiled to the Andaman Islands. British soldiers from the Dorset regiment, who came to fight the rioters also perished.

The atrocities were endless on all sides. In one instance sixty-one out of ninety prisoners being transported to *Podanur,* on their way to the Coimbatore jail, one hundred-and twenty kilometres away, in a windowless wagon without food or water, died during the journey. This is often referred to as the *Jallianwala Bagh* incident of Malabar. Many of the rioters were banished to the Andaman Islands and never returned. The British soldiers who died are remembered in a brass plaque at Saint Mark's Cathedral, Bangalore.

The influence of Saudi Arabia began to spread in Malabar after the exodus to the Gulf countries started in the mid-twentieth century. This has made a significant change in the attitude of some of the Muslims in Malabar and elsewhere. The men brought home large amounts of money as well as a stricter form of religion (Wahabi) from the Gulf. Now, in Kerala, some women wear the hijab and some even go as far as to wear those long *burkhas* that cover all except the eyes.

12

The house – my home till I was fifteen. Three bedrooms in a line, all opening on to a narrow entrance corridor with a cow-dung floor. In front, a veranda that wrapped round two sides of the house. Upstairs replicated the three rooms and a corridor motif. The women lived downstairs and Achan majestically, all alone, as befitted his status as the wage-earner, upstairs in the corridor. I percolated up and down. All the bedrooms downstairs had cow-dung floors. My cousin Naani re-painted the floor with fresh cow dung twice a month on Fridays and before festival days.

For me, cow dung day was special. First, Devi would be sent off to pick up cow dung from the road in front of our house. Then Naani would pound some of the charcoal from our hearth to mix into the dung to tone down the greenish colour of fresh dung. She would do the painting of the floor late at night when everyone had gone to bed, because it would need a good four or five hours to dry. I would hang about full of expectation, and if I behaved myself, she would give me a little of the dung-and-water mixture in a coconut shell. I was allowed to do corners. After the work was done, she would heat water for our baths on the three-stone hearth in a corner of our bathroom and we would bathe together; I loved that woman.

The little land around the house had a Jack tree, nine anaemic coconut trees and some banana trees. The banana trees were planted by Achamma and we used the fruit, but the landlord came every now and then to collect a harvest of coconuts. The Jack fruit was plucked early and used for curries. Naani made curries with the fruit in many different ways: with tamarind and ground coconut, dry roasted with curry pastes, and coconut sprinkled on top. She even used the seeds to fry in oil or roast on the wood-fire, though I was frequently warned that seeds would lead to smelly farts. I knew from experience that she was right, but I could not resist the seeds, fried or roasted on hot embers.

The plantains were also used for curries made with dhal. Naani would fry grated coconut, cumin and shallots for flavouring at the end. This is still a favourite dish of mine.

Behind the house, and tucked away in a corner was the latrine, one room for men and one for women. The women's room had a door and the men's room was wide open to the elements. It was at the far end and women and girls did not go in that direction. A man from the untouchable caste, the *Parayas*, would come early every morning to empty the shit pot. If he was a little late, Achamma would get quite incensed: she claimed that her day would be full of bad luck if she saw the shit carrier first thing in the morning.

There was a deep gully behind the house; this separated our house from the one behind, which I visited daily. Someone had put a line of large red bricks down so that we didn't need to touch the filthy gully with our bare feet. This worked well in the dry season, but during the monsoons, the rainwater would come tumbling down from *Pallikunnu*, the hill above our houses. Then the gully would be a turbulent, narrow river rushing down like a rapid, and I would stand at the edge and watch all the things that came down: banana tree trunks, broken shit pots and turd, and from further up, dead, bloated goats and palm fronds.

Sometimes it was a woman who came to empty the shit pot; I always felt sorry for her. When the men lifted the shit pot on to their shoulders, I didn't feel particularly sad for them. The woman who came was lovely -- she had a beautiful smile and it would break out like sunshine every time you engaged with her. She would often come over to the back of the house to ask for a drink. Maathu, our maid, would be sent to deal with her because nobody in the kitchen would go near her.

'Stay away,' Ammamma would instruct me, but I would sneak out. 'She'll stink,' Ammamma would add. Actually she was always neatly dressed in a short half-sari, and looked clean; she never stank.

Maathu did not like going near her, so she would stand at some distance and pour the conjee water for her from a long spout.

Isn't Molu going to school today?' the woman would ask if I was anywhere near.

'Later,' I would answer.

'Strange tribe,' Achamma said about the Parayas.

There was a vacant plot at the end of our road and the Parayas had established camp there. Achamma said they were promiscuous, the woman and the men. She had no evidence for this of course; it was an assumption born out of contempt. Achamma's definition of promiscuity, in any case, included looking at a man for more than a minute.

Mani and I were curious about these people who were not allowed into society – the untouchables. We would sneak off to the south end of the large compound, part of the Echiveedu, our house of sisters where we often visited to look at their animals and hens, and if we parted the *Yeshoda* creepers at the fence, we could see the Paraya men and women going about their daily lives.

The men sat around (now, there's a surprise) and the women would be sweeping around the camp, pounding something in their mortars or washing clothes The Parayas had chosen that spot because there was an old well there and lots of land to use as latrine.

One day, deep into the night, I was woken up by the sound of drums, muffled, coming from the empty land. '*Parayas* cavorting,' Ammamma said. Mani and I were *curiouser and curiouser* after that, so we often went over to sneak a look. We were rewarded quite soon. One afternoon we parted that fence in the house behind ours – two men were beating a quick rhythm on drums and men and women were dancing in a circle. They clapped their hands to a chant, which we couldn't quite catch. We could hear loud laughter and occasionally some women joined in the chant.

A drink was being distributed from a big clay pot; the woman near the pot dipped a half-coconut shell into the pot as men and women came up for refills. Some of the men and women were staggering around, clearly drunk; we had never seen a woman drink and this was amazing. In a far corner of the plot a calf was being slaughtered and cut up into large chunks. Nearby a fire was raging in what looked like a pit with logs over it. That event carried on for three days; we could hear the drums.

We never told anyone at home what we saw. The women and men, happy together, enjoying the event – I had never seen women celebrate like this. The women in our lives seemed, in comparison, to live joyless lives. So respectability, I thought, was a strange culture: fun only for men, who could do what they wanted, while the women stayed at home, cooked and cleaned, fasted and prayed for the men. They were not encouraged to enjoy themselves.

My father was active in promoting equal access for the untouchables to temples and public places. This was the declared creed of the Congress Party and its de-facto leader, Mahatma Gandhi, and my father was fully committed to this, both by inclination as well as his allegiance to his party. He was vociferous in fighting for the rights of all castes, including the Parayas. These battles, started during the freedom campaign, had a long way to run, and would reach fruition only after independence.

13

Generally, Achamma's favourite time was at dusk when the nilavilakku, the puja lamp in the padinjitta (central room) was lighted. If she suspected evil pursuing a member of our household, she knew the remedies. It was her job to ward off the evil eye, in particular.

She would fill a betel leaf with fresh peppercorns, dry red chilli beans, salt, hibiscus petals, the Thulasi (a variety of Basil) leaves used for worship, and sacred ash. A wick dipped in coconut oil would be carefully tucked into the pointed end of the leaf, which she would shape like a shell, and the wick would be lighted. I never found out exactly what she chanted after this because it was a mumble under her breath. This was the moment when she exorcised all the evil spirits from her home. And from any child who had the temerity to hover near her.

She would wave her magical betel leaf three times in front of my face if it was me she was saving from misfortunes. In those years just before she died, I was always being 'saved' as I was thin and sickly-looking. I had a cough every night, which worried my father because my mother had died of Tuberculosis. After the *mantram* (magic chant) I would be instructed to blow the little flame. Then she would rush to the kitchen to throw the whole concoction on the open fire; if it spluttered noisily,

112

the betel-magic had worked.

I found her a cold woman; she never engaged in a conversation with any of us children, and spent most of her time in bed. Ammamma would call her out at meal-times and she would creep out for a brief moment at dusk to do her prayers and incantations.

In 1942, however, Achamma's life disintegrated around her. My father was arrested and spirited away to some unknown jail. She thought jail happened only to criminals; once the prisoners were taken there, they would be tortured, maybe killed. It was all incomprehensible. She stopped her evening prayers and spent even more time in her bed, but now with her face turned to the wall.

I remember the day when the Circle-Inspector of Police, Latif, visited, with portentous news, a week before my father was arrested; the house had already hunkered down for the night. It was all hush-hush. He was not a close friend of my father to visit whenever it pleased him. In Achamma's book, people visiting late at night meant only one thing: someone had died in her village about four miles from town, and this was a messenger bearing bad news.

I woke up when I heard knocking on the front door; I also wondered who had died, but all my own people who I cared about were well and in our house, so I was not worried. I was cold-blooded about the rest of the world out there. No one had a phone anywhere in the village or even on our road at that time; we didn't have electricity either. Messengers of the night usually came waving a *chootah* (a long flare made out of dry coconut frond tied together and lighted at the leaf-end.)

By the time Ammamma pulled the wooden front door open and rolled it back ponderously, I was wide awake, ready to listen in. I saw Achan stumble out of bed and sit upright. He scratched his chest-hair as he often did when thoughtful, and tightened his white lungi, on his thin waist; skeletal as he was, he had a tough time holding a lungi together.

When Latif reached the long upstairs corridor in which my father and I slept, he seemed diffident. Not the Latif who came to our house occasionally to play the card-game, *twenty-eight*, and roar with boyish hoots when he had brought off a clever trick. He looked sober, deflated.

'The list has come, Raghava,' he said, without preamble. 'Your name is the first on it.' I had no idea what this list was meant to be.

Achan called out to Ammamma to bring the lantern, which was always parked in the corridor downstairs on a low flame.

'No. No light,' Latif said. 'It's all meant to be confidential. I sneaked a look when the Superintendent was out of the room.'

'Eda (boy, used mainly between friends), you could lose your job,' my father remarked. 'Are there many on that list?'

'Three in all,' Latif answered, but he didn't mention any more names. 'I better go.' He sounded uncertain.

'How much time do I have?' Achan persisted.

'Depends on the All India Congress Party Conference coming up in Wardha. They say Gandhi will ask the British to quit India. If the resolution gets passed, you'll have to go in a day or two.'

114

Achan got back into bed, but he stayed awake a long while after, staring at the ceiling, and I looked at him in the half-light of the moon. The index finger on his right hand was resting on his nose; my father's normal response when he heard bad news. The shadows of coconut palm-leaves outside, moving in the wind, danced on the wall and I saw phantoms and portents.

Many years later, Achan told me about the unfinished business attached to his arrest. He, with some friends, had been planning to remove the Union Jack flying over the Court buildings, at night, and replace it with a Tricolour, orange, white and green, with a charkha, Gandhi's spinning wheel, in the middle. Did the police come to know about it? Had someone informed on them?

The All India Congress Committee met at the Gowalia Tank Maidanam, Bombay, on 8th August, 1942. Gandhi introduced the Quit India resolution, which was passed unanimously. The Stafford Cripps mission had come and gone in March 1942; Congress not only rejected it, it made them frustrated and angry at being treated like children, at a time when the Japanese were knocking at the door, and Indians were joining the British army in thousands.

Gandhi's message to Indians was '*do or die.*' The government declared The Indian National Congress and its four regional committees illegal and all the members were arrested; with the leadership sequestered, demonstrations, some violent, broke out in the streets all over India.

When news reached us in Thalassery on 9th August the tempo of the house changed; Achan called Ammamma upstairs to talk to her. He then rushed off into town. When Ammamma went back to the kitchen, she looked distraught and angry at the same time. She shouted at the maid, Maathu.

'What are you staring at?' she asked. Maathu picked up a broom and walked out into the yard, swinging it to brush the floor lightly.

'The child is motherless, now she will be fatherless as well,' Ammamma muttered.

Actually, for me, not having a mother was a non-event. There were enough proxy mothers in our household and I felt loved by all. But Achan? A small nagging worry made me cling to Ammamma, who hadn't noticed me hovering in the background. And what was this precious list that was causing such havoc. Was it like a dhobi list? I wondered.

What's happening to Achan?' I asked Ammamma.

'Nothing. Go away. Haven't you got homework to do?'

Clearly, no answers were forthcoming from this source. I wandered off and found Mani, my cousin, always a little ahead of news in the house. But she admitted she didn't know either.

That evening I confronted father in bed. He had his bedside lamp on behind the bed and his face was in the shadow.

'Yesterday...' I began.

'Yes, yesterday.' He closed the thin booklet he was reading. It was a collection of poems by various *Malayalee* poets.

'You should read this book too,' he said, as he replaced it carefully in the small revolving bookcase behind his bed.

'Yesterday,' I began again. 'Ammamma says you are not going to be here. And I'm going to be fatherless. That's not true, is it?'

He put his arm out and ruffled my hair.

'I have to go away for a little while, but I'll be back soon. You know I always come back.' I didn't like the sound of this. It wasn't 'I'll be in before dark,' or 'soon as the case is over.'

'Go where?'

He didn't answer. 'Go to sleep,' he said instead.

I sensed a siege atmosphere in the house in the coming weeks after Latif's visit Achan pulled out all the drawers in the chest at the end of the corridor where he slept. He picked some clothes and put them aside. He also stared out of the window a great deal, lost in thought.

At one point he called Ammamma upstairs and gave her a bundle of rupee notes.

'One thousand four hundred and a bit,' he said. 'This will have to last till I come back.'

'And when is that?' Ammamma looked angry and dismayed.

Achan stayed silent. He shook his head as though throwing out a bad thought.

'I was going to buy a small piece of land on this road and build a house for us.'

'Why do you have to be the one going?' Ammamma insisted angrily. There was no answer to that. In my head, I was asking the same question. 'Lots of men around with wives, who can look after the children – why is it always you?' she insisted.

When she left he examined the bookshelf on the wall and extracted two huge tomes: The complete

Works of Bernard Shaw and the Indian Penal Code.

'Quantity rather than quality,' he said, smiling.

I smelled the leather of old binding.

'These will last me a while,' he said as I hung around, putting my hands into the bottom shelf, sniffing at the musty books and getting in his way. He pulled out an old leather suitcase from the junk room next door and asked Naani Edathy to polish the rusting catches.

This was just the kind of day I really loved, when all sorts of unnameable objects got scattered about the rooms and adults were too busy to notice what I was doing. With Achan safely occupied in the junk room and Naani Edathy busy with a tin-lid containing kerosene, and a rag, I sneaked off in the direction of Achan's precious chest-of-drawers. No one went anywhere near it and he always carried the keys to it tucked into his *mundu* (white sarong-like garment) at the waist. However, I knew that some drawers were never locked.

The bottom drawers had no locks and I knew they contained old papers, and clothes, which Achan never wore. I pulled the drawer out slowly; A strong smell of mothballs escaped. The drawer was heavy and did not roll out easily; it stuck halfway. I put my arm in and moved things about, feeling rather than seeing much. Something soft and silky, then something metallic. I pulled out some stuff willy-nilly. What a treasure trove!

The silky objects were old, cream, silk *lungis* that velyachan had brought for Achan from Malaya, on one of his visits. He wore then for a few days, then put them away, as they kept slipping off his meagre waist. The silver soap tray in there was my mother's;

later I would claim it for myself, but now it contained small white-and-gold conch-shaped shells, the size of orange seeds – what were they for? An old-fashioned, kidney-shaped baby-bottle nestled among a pair of flannel shorts. The bottle, I knew had been mine. Later, I would use it to feed my first son, Kitta, when he was born in 1958. But flannel shorts? Whose were they, and what for?

Papers were boring, but there was a browning old roll, wrapped in yellowing newspaper, at the right side of the drawer. What could that be? I pulled it out gently and unrolled it without making a noise. It was an A3 sized sepia photo of a young woman. I had a good look; I took it out and laid it on the bed nearby, holding it flat with my elbow and my arm. It rustled and the edges looked fragile. It was formal-looking, the woman didn't smile. The picture meanwhile kept rolling back loosely denying me a proper view of the woman; it smelt of camphor and dried newspaper.

I decided the paper would stay flat if I rolled it inside out, so I did that. The edges felt brittle, in danger of crumbling. This was the moment caution escaped through the nearest window; the photo rustled and cracked at the edges, and Achan walked in.

'What?' he said in disbelief. He rushed over and seized the picture from me, rolling it up gently as he walked over to his bureau and placed it inside.

'Who was that woman?' I asked. My father looked nonplussed.

'Your mother,' he said briefly, not looking at me.

'Can I have another look?' I ventured, not very hopefully.

119

'Not now – another time.' He said. 'Maybe.'

Looking at the expression on Achan's face, I had enough seven-year-old wit to stop asking and make my escape.

After that, whenever Achan opened the bottom drawer of his chest-of-drawers in my presence, I put on my most winsome look, but Achan ignored me. I never saw that picture after that until Achan died when I was forty-eight years old. It didn't appear any more damaged than it had been when I was only seven.

They came for Achan on a Thursday, very early one morning in August 1942, when the people in the houses that edged the road were still busy on their back-verandas cleaning teeth with coal-dust or burnt rice-husk. The Cunnoor bus hurtled past swaying a little as it dodged to the side to overtake a shit-cart. A pie-dog snuffled around; the milkman's bicycle bell proclaimed that another harmless day was getting into gear.

A jeep stopped in front of our gates and two men in police uniform tumbled out. They looked right and left as they opened our gate. There was a hierarchy there – the one behind carried the bag and the one in front flicked his beedi on to our *Touch-me-nots*.

Achan was shaving in front of a small shaving mirror, strategically placed on the window-sill; his chin was lathered up, and he was squinting and grimacing into the mirror, as men do when trying to get the difficult bits round their mouths. I was standing near him, looking out the window. I liked hanging around near him when he was in the house and in a good mood; when he was grumpy, all of us three children disappeared downstairs out of his way. His bad temper was usually loud, unreasonable and smouldering, and the person who was unlucky enough to be near him when it got to a head, generally got the brunt of it.

'Policukaran,' I said.

Achan stopped lathering his face, put down the brush in the shaving mug and looked out too.
The men walked warily looking right and left at the houses on either side of ours.

On the road, a mad man came around picking paper and banana skin from the side of the road, depositing them neatly in the middle. He muttered to himself as he worked his way down the road.

'*Pranthan Achu*,' I said. Everyone knew our own madman, especially the boys like Appuettan who threw stones at him when adults weren't looking.

In the front-yard, Maathu, our maid, was slowly sweeping the yard, bent over a short broom made of coconut fronds, making lazy half-circles. Periodically she straightened up and arched her torso backwards.

Achan quickly wiped his face with his shaving towel and told me to go downstairs. I did not move. A little lather sat on his ear-lobe. He peeped quickly into the junk room and pulled a vest on. He extracted a khadi *jubba* (long, collarless, tunic like shirt) and mundu, from his chest-of-drawers and slipped them on quickly. I didn't say anything, filled with some nameless foreboding. Meanwhile, the policemen had arrived upstairs.

The bag-carrier was looking anywhere except at my father's face.

'Entha,' Achan asked, and he was looking at me.

The man-in-charge nodded towards my father and the minion pulled out a pair of handcuffs from his bag. Achan flinched.

'No need for that,' he said. His voice sounded a little strangled. 'Let me get my stuff.'

'Moley – go to Ammamma,' Achan said to me but I wasn't budging.

The man with the handcuffs looked at my father's thin, white wrists, and put the cuffs away in his bag.

Ammamma came up the stairs then, sounding even more flat-footed than usual. Slap, slap, slap...

'They walked in before I could get the front the door half-open,' she began. Then she stopped, staring at the scene in front of her.

Achan signalled to her a trifle impatiently. 'Take this child downstairs with you.' She tugged at me gently, but I shook her off. What were they going to do to my Achan? For once he seemed not to be in control.

'Go,' Achan said to me. There was no give in his tone. So I slunk off and waited at the bottom of the stairs.

Achamma's bedroom was on the left near where I stood. She was sitting up in bed a little groggily.

'*Aaraa*?' Who is it?

'Policukaran,' I answered. Achamma's feet dangled above the floor but she would not put them down and get up. Meanwhile the women in the house were all gathered in the corridor, Appuettan at the back with Naaniedathy and Mani in front.

When Achan reached the bottom of the stairs he put his head under the low wooden lintel of his mother's room and spoke to her. 'I'm going,' he said, uncertainly.

She put her feet up on the bed, laid down and turned to the wall.

'Ammey,' he pleaded, but she would not budge. He stood, looking at her for a moment. For once, my Achan, always full of words, seemed to have none.

I flung myself at Achan and put my arms round his legs.

'Tell these men to go, away,' I said. Mani came forward then. 'Elayacha –'she began. He knelt down then and gathered both of us together.

'Look after each other,' he said. 'No crying.' So we stood back and the men marched him off to the waiting jeep.

A few local people had, by this time, gathered round the jeep. As Achan got in, they crowded closer. The bag-carrier looked uneasy.

Achan turned to one or two neighbours who crowded near the rear of the jeep.

'Better not start anything. It will only make matters worse for me – and you.' They retreated slowly as the jeep started up and drove down the hill.

Mani and I, meanwhile, were hanging around the gate, watching the excitement. Kannettan, our neighbour, who lived behind us, told us to go away; he seemed rattled, but he was always a little stressed and screwing up his face; that was nothing unusual. We went back to Ammamma who was standing on the veranda.

'He'll come back in the evening,' I said.

That night, and until my father returned from jail two years later, I slept in Ammamma's bed, which smelled of the hibiscus leaves she pounded and used for shampoo in her hair, not the Pears soap

123

that Achan used. Her bed was spartan, not soft like Achan's. There was a grass mat at the bottom and a thin mattress above it. I curled myself into her back; which always felt warm. Achan never let me sleep that close unless I had a nightmare. Then he would talk to me and rest his arm on me.

'Wake me up when he comes,' I told her. 'Sure,' she said, and hugged me.

That was strange – Ammamma never hugged anyone.

14

I am paranoid about access to food. I wonder whether people here in Britain, who lived through the war, are also, like me, insecure in this respect. Or, have the good years in between erased that memory? I'm sure it is the result of living through the fallow years in Thalassery when Achan was in jail. These days it manifests itself in the amounts of food I cook each day; it is always too much and my daughter grumbles as she searches for plastic boxes to put the food away. And curses even more when we have to eat the old food the next day so it is not wasted.

My father had gone to jail in 1942 because he did not approve of the British Government and wanted them to quit India. He was one of the many men and women arrested immediately after the *Quit India* resolution was passed in August, 1942. Above all, India did not want to be part of a war, on which they had not been consulted. The activists who were detained were not released for two years; no one knew where they had been taken or when they would come back.

My father had a strong personality, which led rather than followed. So he had been ideal for this time, in this little town, Thalassery, to rally the public, make impassioned speeches in Malayalam and English, organise meetings and processions, and in general get under the skin of the paranoid coloniser.

The dreaded Section 144 had been declared by a colonial government in sheer panic, sometime before, and meetings of more than five people in public were banned by decree. The party members met in the houses of activists and in the quiet corners of local beaches, where they could look like ordinary people enjoying the evening. In these gatherings, there were some policemen too and no one was concerned that they would be reported to the authorities.

I was often carrying glasses of water or tea out to the men when the meetings were in our house. Ammamma complained about the way the milk ran out early in the evening and she had to make coffee laced with ghee and lots of sugar. At the beach, I ran around with the children of some of the other activists. This became the new normal. When, in the end, they were all rounded up and went to jail, I was just over seven years old.

My father was the only bread-winner in our household. There was myself, my two cousins not much older than me, Ammamma, Naani and Achamma to be fed. Naani cooked whatever there was to cook: mainly moong in many enterprising ways and rice three times a day. Morning and evening, it was *rice-conjee* in its liquid cooking starch, and afternoons it appeared as rice with a catch-all curry called Sambhar, into which dhal and all kinds of suspicious leaves and vegetables went. It was tasty and I love it still. A lot of love went into it

126

because Naani knew how to love.

At the end of the day, there would not be much food left for Naani, the cook. I would find her scraping the bottom of the rice pan with her hands to get a decent serving. Scraping gently, and not with the *kayyil,* the large serving spoon made from a half-coconut shell.

I asked her once. 'Why aren't you using the *kayyil*?
'We don't want the neighbours to know the way it is. It is a lawyer's house; there should not be a food-shortage here.' She was only fifteen years old then; how did she arrive at that sense of status of an absent lawyer?

Now, in our Great Britain, in 2017, when I see those empty fridges and larders in the homes of single mothers, I am appalled. Where did the *great*-ness go? So many young mothers are forced to go to the food-bank for just enough food to feed their children; I feel a tremendous sense of failure. I cannot believe that a Government, even a Tory Government, in 2017, can allow this to happen. Europe is flourishing, they say, and America is rapidly regaining its swagger. And we are supposed to be the sixth richest country in the world. Where are those riches going? And who is responsible for this terrible inequality? Why has this ridiculous government abrogated its duty to its less rich people?

Looking back to the years 1942-1944, when my father was away, the children of the house were always well-fed and nurtured. Luxury was not within reach; our clothes were thread-bare and faded, food was basic and we did not go to cinemas or any form of entertainment. But we were never hungry.

However, when we outgrew our school-garments, Naani Edathy would cut them up and make her blouses with them, because whatever little money there was, went to meeting the needs of Appuettan, Mani and I. Mani's father used to send remittances for them until the Japanese occupation of Singapore; after that, for many years, there were no letters or money.

Electricity had not reached us in 1943 and we depended on kerosene lamps. But, when the war started, kerosene was in short supply and rationed. We had three lamps for the whole house, upstairs and downstairs – a hurricane lantern, a lamp with a long glass funnel, and a minute lamp the size of a large egg. Indeed it was called *Muttavilakku*, egg-lamp. This was reserved for the kitchen and generally stood on the hearth, above the wood fires, except when Naaniedathy was chopping vegetables. Then, it would be on the floor beside her cutting board.

The lantern sat in the veranda and we children did our homework by it. It didn't manage to give enough light to all three children, so I remember I would often furtively nudge the lantern slightly towards me. It didn't go down well with the other two. The tall lamp was father's and was rarely used when he was not at home. The reason was simple – the kerosene allowed our household did not run to the luxury of three lamps, however tiny or dim. You could buy kerosene in the black market in the back of the ration stores, where there was always a brisk clandestine trade in rationed goods – sugar, rice and kerosene, but we could not afford it. When anyone moved around the house we carried the lantern in our hands.

With the war an *'Ayarpee'* (ARP) man turned up every evening to make sure we had no lights showing for the Japanese planes to see down below. He was in the ARP uniform of short khaki trousers and white shirt and he wore it with pride.

'Must close all the curtains,' he would say. We didn't have a single curtain in the house, so Ammamma would let that pass. Indeed we never possessed a door or window curtain until the week of my wedding, when some kind friend, brought two huge bales of maroon net and draped every window. It didn't last long – father took it down the day after the wedding saying it would encourage spider webs and pests; neighbours borrowed the curtains for their own weddings and such-like. That set of curtains did the rounds at many events in that road. Somewhere along the line, they disappeared, forgotten in a house down the road, but no one remembered which house had last borrowed it. And today, every window in our house in Purley is draped in curtains, carefully chosen for aesthetic value. What a sea-change considering my origins. Where did the Thoreau-esque simplicity disappear?

In any case, the ARP man came also for a hot cup of tea and a chat, so he would sit on the bench on the veranda, which tilted, and came down with a resounding thud if you sat at one end. Ammamma and he would exchange the news of the day. Who had black market rice? Who was getting married and needed sugar in large quantities? He would sigh.

'Getting married in war-time, for heaven's sake!' Ammamma agreed.

129

Ammamma worried about many other things -- worry was her default mood in those days, when Achan was away. Many days she would take her pan-box and sit on the rickety bench on the veranda just behind my corner on the steps. She kept her small change in the bottom compartment of the box; I would see her counting her coins again and again as though they would increase by counting.

One day, Naani Edathy joined her on that bench.

'Fees,' Ammamma ventured.

'There is no money for school fees next month. Maybe the girls can stop school for a little while.'

They must have forgotten I was there.

'Raghavan said the children must continue at school whatever happens when he gave me his savings.' Ammamma continued. 'What's the point in educating girls? I can't see.' She was appealing to Naani edathy to approve of what she was suggesting.

I did not like what I was hearing. I am a good student; I like school. Why do we have to stop and not Appu ettan? I thought.

Ammamma had her answers.

'Boys, I can understand. Girls will just marry and go to someone else's house. They need to cook and clean and know how to live with their mother-in-law.

'We managed without, you and I, didn't we?'

Nani Edathy guffawed.

'And look at us. No money, no education, no husbands. We did great, didn't we?'

Ammamma closed the pan-box with a bang and went inside. 'Just talk,' Naani Edathy said to me. 'She won't do anything.'

Financially, even I could see we were limping along.

130

Ammamma tried to grow vegetables in the garden and managed some sad-looking corns. This was one of the 'Grow More Food' slogans of the war, asking us *Malayalees* to eat corn and wheat, because there was a shortage of rice.

Having grown corn, Ammamma had no idea what to
do with it. She soaked it and boiled it like rice and eventually gave it to the maid.

The ration shop gave all households a small amount of wheat to supplement the insufficient rice allowance – eight ounces per person per day. In those days wheat was not something that we, Malayalees, normally cooked. But Naani Edathy soaked it and cooked it with a little moong and rice and made a conjee out of it, which was quite eatable. Occasionally, if we grumbled, she added a spoonful of grated coconut to make it richer. Sometimes she gave us pieces of jaggery to make it sweet. There were days when there was no rice at all in the conjee and it would be just moong and wheat. We hated it and invented ways to get rid of it without Naaniedathy noticing. One that worked sometimes was to dump the moong-wheat mixture into the brass tumblers in which drinking water was served to us.

Chappathis were another matter altogether. The women tried making chappathis, but having never made them before, or indeed eaten them, this fizzled out as well. The chappathis were uneatable, like dusty cardboard. Strangely, some households persisted and eventually, chappathis became a part of South Indian cuisine. Today, even I, not famous for my cooking skills, can make chappathis.

Achan's youngest sister, Dechooty, helped in

many ways. She lived on a farm in our village, Moozhikkara, and she would often send us rice, plantains, bananas, coconuts and Jack-fruit to supplement our meagre war-time rations. They were smuggled under old clothes, on the head of a woman farm-worker, as the movement of rice from farm to people directly, was not allowed. The harvest had to be declared to the Government and sold to them for next-to-nothing. Inspectors went to the houses of farmers and audited their harvest many times in a year. So, the black market flourished, and my aunt found novel ways of hiding her harvest and getting it to us. She also helped us by lending us one of her sons to live with us and provide man-support in a houseful of women. She had six sons and three of them came almost in rotation. One, Keshavan, stuck, and we appropriated him forever.

So many people helped us to get through those years. Neighbours offered us their sugar rations, tailors did sewing for nothing and fruits and buns arrived frequently from various households. When Ammamma demurred saying she shouldn't accept their scant rations, our neighbour, Madhavi, insisted that they had diabetes in their house and could not use the sugar.

Ammamma stared hard at her.

'Don't give diseases to people who don't have it,' she said. 'God will not like it.'

Ammamma spent so many hours in front of our household shrine she was sure she had a direct link to the almighty's thinking.

Madhavi thought for a moment before saying:
'Vakil (lawyer) went to jail for all of us, so all of us have to help.

15

I did not know whether to be proud of my father or just plain sad. Or annoyed. The nuns at school added to my confusion. I can't claim I was a perfectly behaved girl – far from it. But I generally managed to kick Moosa, who sat on the front bench, next to me in class, on the shin, when he put snot on my book without Sister Nympha noticing. Girija was another matter; she was a source of continuous angst, though she was also my friend. She had lovely waist-length hair and Mani and I were not allowed to have long hair; I was jealous. Achan insisted that we should not grow our hair long until we knew how to care for it. As in no lice, no knots like birds' nests, no dandruff, no grease.

Mani was good at all this: she had no lice ever and looked perfectly groomed always. In fact, growing up with this example of perfect girl-hood was a strain on my rather more careless attitude to grooming. I was a disaster; lice proliferated and no amount of combing them out would get rid of them. My hair always looked a mess, the slides that Achan brought to keep it out of my eyes got lost in a morning, and teachers in school threatened to tie coir rope on my head. So Achan decreed short hair for us both. Unfair on Mani, so he generally allowed her an inch or two extra length of hair.

There were no hairdressing salons, stylists and such other special beauticians in Thalassery in the forties or fifties. So a barber shop was where Achan took the two of us. Even in Kochi, the first hair-salon was set up only in the late nineties by a Japanese lady, who was married to an Indian. Mani would cry right through the hair-cutting day until her face was smeared with snot mixed with copious angry tears; there were never any girls but us in the barber shop and the barber would try to comfort Mani by giving her a little extra length of hair, beyond his instructions from my father. I would feel seriously culpable.

To this day, with both of us in our eighties, she still manages to look perfectly groomed and I end up looking frayed and dishevelled. Especially when I am standing next to her. Her hair is long, plaited and coiled into a neat *konda* (bun) at the nape; her gold chains hang round her neck, diamond pendants dazzling as they catch the light; her sari is perfectly pleated and stays so to the end of the day, even after an afternoon siesta. And I? The less said the better. Something in the genes?

Hair is a serious issue to all Indian girls; in my childhood girls grew their hair from about the age of six or seven; Mani and I felt quite deprived. All the girls in our class had hair at least shoulder length; the sight of it could bring my atavistic instincts exploding to the surface. Moosa who sat next to me on my left, on the front bench, in class, of course had cropped hair. Girija, on the other hand, who sat on my right, had seriously provocative hair. She was a pretty girl, in contrast to me – my hair was so short I looked like a boy, and was Sister's first choice when there was a boy's part to fill in a school drama. So, in turn, I was the heroin's young brother in *Basket of Flowers*, David in David and Goliath...

Girija had two waist-length plaits down her back with red ribbons at the end. We were good friends and occasionally traded bangles and necklaces. Once I exchanged my gold chain for her red bead-chain that I coveted. Ammamma had to make a humongous fuss to make me understand that I had to get my gold chain back; it was not the same as the bead-chain. I kept telling Ammamma Girija's beads were a lot prettier. I thought I had got the better of the bargain. So, you could say we had form.

What irritated me that particular day was Girija's smugness. Some brother had come back from East Africa after three years, bearing gifts, among them hair baubles for Girija. I had seen nothing like this ever in Thalassery. Shining bobby-pins with rhinestones sparkling on their end; broad, satin ribbons and artificial roses. For a week, she had been talking about nothing else. On that day when I came to the end of my hair-patience, she had arranged her two plaits in front of her on either shoulder, so we couldn't miss them. She chose the wrong day – I had had my hair cut, again, just the weekend before. And I looked like a boy -- again. So I did what any self-respecting little girl would do face-to-face with this kind of hair-challenge. When she leaned forward to write something in her notebook, I pulled the plaits back gently, untied the knots on her ribbons and tied them to the slats of the bench behind her.

Sister Nympha chose that moment to ask her a question. It was fractions that day and sister had exhausted her entire mathematical toolkit; she didn't have much anyway. She had gone on about top numbers and bottom numbers, frothing and spitting as she always did when she got excited, and getting comprehensively muddled. Girija had made the mistake of grinning seeing sister's discomfiture.

'If you are so clever, Girija, perhaps you could tell us whether you think two over three is two divided by three, or three divided by two.' Girija started to get up, and that's when her hair jerked her back on to the bench and she fell back. Sister looked at my face and guessed what had happened.

'Anandam,' she said. 'You wicked girl. Stand up.' Sister was the authority on all sorts of sins, mortal, venial... She was our Moral Science teacher as well and had a direct access to places like hell, purgatory and Limbo.

'Just like your jailbird father. Don't know the difference between right and wrong.' Sister was apoplectic and her spittle sprayed almost on to Moosa's smirking face. A collective gasp from the class erupted. Fathers, they knew, were sacrosanct, but sister wouldn't know that. She was from Mangalore, what did Mangaloreans know about Kerala taboos?

I started crying. The whole class stared in turns at Sister and me.

'My father went to jail for freedom for us. For all of us. You too, Sister.' The words came out punctuated by angry sobs. I didn't understand a great deal about all of this, but our neighbour, Kannettan, had drilled this into me. 'Be proud of him. He went for all of us, including those women in the convent who think they are *Madammas*.'

136

The nuns, for some unknown reason, favoured the British and did not want India to become independent. Most of them were Anglo-Indians and the British, reciprocally, considered Anglo-Indians to be the most tolerable of the Indians, the closest to themselves.

When the British Government built railways in the states they governed, to help the movement of men and troops, they did not allow Indians to use or drive the trains. Eventually, when they could no longer have British drivers because they were needed at the front in 1942, the government allowed the Anglo-Indians to take over. Thus, train driving became a traditional Anglo-Indian reserve. There was an unspoken nexus between Anglo Indians and the British.

Kannettan was a passionate Congress activist, who had an unfortunate habit of making a peroration out of a passing comment. Since father went to jail, Kannettan did many errands for us, getting our ration books sorted out, doing our marketing sometimes, taking us children to the local temple festival... He even made our new dresses for Mani and me to go with him to the temple, as he was a tailor by profession. So, he'd earned the right.

My outburst seemed to have stunned Sister into silence. She looked down at her text-book, scratched her nose, and when she surfaced she looked shame-faced.

'Back to top-heavy fractions,' she said, staring dismally into some middle-distance of her own. I slowly walked out of the class and sat on the parapet outside, until break, when Girija found me there.

'You can have my red ribbon,' she said.

16

My father was one of three men, leaders, so-called, who were arrested in the first tranche – they were the only professional men arrested from Thalassery, in the mayhem of August, 1942. After this, the leaderless mobs took to the streets in protest; the police pretended not to notice. Later the demonstrations became violent and the police had no choice but to arrest many men. Women now joined the activists.

My ammamma was one of the many women who had never ventured into any form of public debate, who now decided to take up the challenge. A friend down the road, Rohini, organised meetings in her house. We met at her house often. We pasted paper tricolour flags on our blouses and sang the national anthem. Rohini spoke to the small crowd, mainly women, about them having to take over and continue the work that the men had started, because so many men, active in the movement, were now imprisoned.

Rohini teacher, or simply teacher, as she was called affectionately by the neighbourhood, was well-loved and respected in the community. She had married a man from another caste at a time when this was a crime for which she could have been ostracised from her community, the *Thiyas*. Her husband was from the *Kaniyan* caste and a scholar of Sanskrit. They joined the *Brahma Samajam*, an organisation, which believed that caste was a scourge on Hindu society, and encouraged men and women to marry outside their caste.

Rohini was a warrior. She went from house to house on that road, getting the women out. Her neighbour and his many sons, marshalled the chairs for the event, which would be lined up in her small front yard. She spoke without microphones, but her experience as a teacher had taught her to gain and keep attention. She organised small *jathas* (processions) – even I marched in them shouting congress slogans.

Ammamma was persuaded to speak to the women who gathered in Rohini Teacher's house. She had never spoken in public and was terrified, but, with my father's special status in the community, she had no choice but to add her voice to the occasion. I remember that she was sick every time she had to speak; her stomach pains would start in the night before the event. She would chant 'Ramaramarama.' and moan a little. Sometimes she got up from the bed, where I also slept, and went to the kitchen to make a thick concoction from roasted and boiled cumin seed.

Women and children, occasionally shepherded by a stray man, ventured out in little processions, shouting *Mahatma Gandhi ki jai*, *Bhaarat maatha ki jai* and *Congress party*, *Sindabad*. The police turned a blind eye -- the children and women were neighbours and friends.

My one impulse during these years was to somehow reach my father. I had to make sure that he was not being tortured like his mad mother said. I had to

139

ascertain whether he was getting his food, his many cups of coffee, and his blue tin of Capstans Navy Cut cigarettes every day. He was thin, he ate little, he often got pneumonia, he would be destroyed easily.

To begin with, we didn't know where they had taken him. Cunnoor jail, we thought. That was only fourteen miles away, an hour by bus, even less by train; I was hopeful. But friends who worked in the jail said he was not there. News trickled down through prison warders, whose loyalty to the British was suspect. It just took a long time for the information to reach home. Where then?

It did not help that there were various classes of '*deteneus*' as they were named by the Government. Just restrained, not really imprisoned, the word indicated. So, I went on a quest to find the meaning of detenue. I asked Ammamma first. Freedom fighter, she answered -- just like adults, I thought; you ask them the meaning of a small word and they give you a bigger one.

The wife of one of the other three prisoners who were taken at about the same time as my father, managed to locate her husband. She applied and got permission to see their detenue. They were a wealthy business family and had the money to travel to his prison; for us this was not an option.

It was three months before we got a first letter from Achan. He was in Velloor, far away, not the kind of place you could suddenly get up and go to. I looked up Velloor on our map of India in school and it looked unattainable.

The wife who had managed to see her husband paid us a courtesy call.

'He was looking well, a little bored, but well,' she

140

said, referring to her husband. 'They are not locked up or anything. Just can't come home.'

I started feeling more hopeful. And then she spoiled it:

'Some prisoners are locked up, two and three to a cell, and don't get enough food.' How could we know how my father was?

'Lots of men were arrested. I think the doctors and lawyers and teachers are alright. But the other people, labourers and such-like, they are suffering.'

For me, hope came and went.

After three months, a letter arrived. The postman brought it with a sense of occasion, as though he was solely responsible for making it happen. He stood in front of the veranda, where Ammamma had settled in for the morning pan-session, after the fish-man had come and gone, major decisions had been made as to how much rice to cook, which wild leaf to harvest from the garden to go with the rice and fish (if she had bought any, which was rare), and now she could count the money in the bottom compartment of her old, brass, pan-box. On the off-chance that it had increased while she was not looking. This was her 'me-time.'

The postman pulled out the off-white envelope with ceremony. 'Letter from Vakil,' he announced. When he had passed the letter on to Ammamma, he hung around waiting to hear the news in the letter. Ammamma pointedly ignored him until he turned around and loped back to the gate; his shoulders expressed a grievance.

The envelope had *Censored. By order of The Government of India* stamped on it.

Achan's letter was four pages long, but most of it was blanked off with Indian Ink. I held it up to the light to see through the ink, but the blackened places defeated me. Still, now we had an address; we could write to him. We knew where he was.

I wrote to him every week, but I didn't know whether he got the letters. It took a while before we started getting regular letters from Achan. They were written in Malayalam to his sister, and at the end, brief paragraphs in English to me, Mani and Appu ettan. Our letters to him too were inked out in places, he said. We wondered why our letters were censored, considering we were two little girls just saying we missed him, and when was he coming back? Random authority showing off power? Since so much of what we wrote was blacked out, Mani and I started drawing pictures for him instead. Years later, after he died, I found a package of our letters with the drawings, in his bottom drawer, with the sepia photo of my mother he had kept safe all those years

Everything seemed random. Some families applied for and got permission to visit their father or husband in prison. They travelled to Velloor or Tanjore or Cunnoor, and came back, if not happy, at least less distressed. But we could not afford it, so I saw my father only when he was given compassionate parole in the April of 1943.

Achan came, without notice, for two weeks, to see his mother, who was fading rapidly. After he went to jail, she, literally, had turned her face to the wall and decided to die. Through that time, she was also slowly going mad. Her eldest son had died in early youth of small-pox; her second son was in Malaya and there was no news of him from the beginning of hostilities between Britain and Japan. And now her youngest son was in prison. She believed all of them were dead, and she had no time for the daughters who cared for her.

Achamma's idea of a prison was a place where you were starved and beaten up. One morning, she grabbed me by my arm when I was contemplating the day from my usual seat on the veranda steps. She dragged me down the walkway to the front gates and pushed me onto the road.

I didn't understand what this was about. Her claw-like hands clutched my elbows fiercely and her skeletal torso was bent forward.

'Go,' she said giving me a shove. 'Go to your mother's house. There's nothing and nobody for you here.'

I stood on the side of the road and made a circle with my heels in the soft dust, trying to work this out. My mother's family lived in Madras, a good day's journey away by train; how was I meant to go there?

After a moment, she looked left and right down the road and pointed in the direction of the river. A bus hurtled past towards Cunnoor.

'There,' she said. 'See. They've tied your father to the back of the bus and they are beating him. He's thin and weak, they'll kill him.' She gave me a firm nudge.

I was now on the edge of our road, more than a little perplexed. So I dug my heel into the red mud on the side and pivoted round again making another small circle with my toes. Achamma turned and went back to the house. I waited a few moments and walked to the veranda looking right and left. Why was I feeling a little ashamed? I hoped no one next door had noticed this little drama.

I pondered. Then I went looking for Naani Edathy.

'Achamma asked me to go away to my Velyamma's house.' I started crying.

Naani Edathy was spreading *dosha* (a crepe made with rice and black-dhal) mixture on the skillet and the hiss and the yeasty smell reminded me of how much I hated doshas.

'That old woman is raving mad,' Naani Edathy said. She was still looking at the skillet and gently turning the dosha. Not what I wanted from her.

I thrust my thumb into the hole in the waist of my slip and howled.

'I am not going,' I sobbed. 'I'm here.'

Naani Edathy quickly took the skillet off the fire and ran towards me.

'Of course you are. With me. That mad old woman!'

She pulled the corner of her mundu out and cleaned my leaking nose and wiped my cheeks. Then she picked me up and held me close.

'You have charcoal streaks on your face,' she said, smiling. I threw my arms around her neck and nestled close.

'I don't like Dosha,' I said capitalising on her kindness.

'How about I roast a plantain for you when no one is looking?

My little sorrows had vanished by then; I jumped off and went in search of Mani. An unease lingered.

'Did Achamma ask you to go to *your* mother's house?' I asked.

'What? To Penang?' she asked sensibly.

After that I was scared of Achamma and kept my distance even though our ripe bananas, mangoes and jack fruit were stored under her bed. She really did not like offering the goodies to us girls, but Appuettan, her one and only *pauthran*, (son of a son), who would be the person to light the pyre at her cremation, always got fruit from her. Mani and I generally waited in the doorway for *his* generosity, which was sporadic. The family rice box was also in the room, and combined with her Waterbury's Compound and Ayurvedic oils, the room always had a ripe, herby smell.

Achamma got more and more mad and started spitting out her medicines as soon as Ammamma gave them to her – vivid pink and maroon splashes on walls and floor. She had made up her mind: all her sons were gone. As for the women, three of them -- they fed her, washed her and took care of her, but they didn't count.

My Velyachan was in Penang right through the Japanese occupation. His letters stopped coming and the money he sent to the house also stopped about a year into Achan's incarceration.

My father came back from jail on parole in the April of '43. When Achamma saw him, she refused to talk to him. She insisted it was her son's ghost and he was long dead. She turned her body to the wall and curled up like a prawn; she died a few months later. I think she made up her mind to die and resisted the efforts to treat her. My father applied for

145

parole again for her funeral but was refused.

The two weeks when he came home on parole were precious. For me, that was the first time I realised my father no longer belonged to me. When I went to school, there would already be a crowd of ten or twelve men crowding around him on the veranda, asking questions, almost basking in the penumbra of his halo. All I could do was peek through the crowd of followers, hoping to get a quick smile or nod.

I complained bitterly to Naani Edathy; she tried to console me. 'He's a leader to them now, but you are the one who sleeps in his bed, and you know he loves you.'

That was not enough; I felt abandoned. That sense of abandonment by someone, for unknown reasons, has stayed with me all my life, like a subcutaneous ache that will not go away. It faded and flared depending on who was with me and how much time they had for me.

Achamma withdrew from the world deliberately, in stages. To begin with, she stopped coming out of her room except for quick meals. She would walk to the latrine and back very early at about seven in the morning.

Then Achamma started staying in her room and food was taken in to her. After eating, she would lie down again, pull up the bed-clothes and turn to the wall. The doctors prescribed medicines for her; all they did was decorate the walls in her room. A commode was found so that she never went out of her room. The much-trodden-upon outside maid, Maathu, now had to empty and wash the filthy pan daily.

Gradually Achamma started muttering and murmuring to herself. She wept copiously. 'They've killed all my sons,' she moaned.

Doctor Shenoy came and went. One day she got a fever and went absolutely quiet. Her left hand was puffed up and pink; the skin was so tight on the palm, it looked like it would split. The doctor came again and looked at her inflamed hand and took her temperature.

'Just watch her,' he said. I touched her forehead – it was burning.

The whole family gathered around her bed and we gave her drops of *Thulasi* water – water in which the sacred basil leaves had been soaked. Her breath was so soft Ammamma could not know whether she was dead or not. So Ammamma held a small mirror to her nostrils. There was nothing on it.

A strangely gentle death. They laid her out on the floor in front of the nilavilakku and neighbours came to pay their respects. Then she was carried away to her village on a bamboo stretcher. All of us followed in a *jutka* and stayed in the village for fourteen days of the initial daily rituals. When we returned, I did not notice her absence or feel any sense of loss.

My father never got over the fact that he had applied for parole and was turned down – an unnecessary cruelty. All his life after, he thought it was he who was responsible for her dying.

17

Meanwhile, as the months passed, Ammamma's little nest-egg, which my father had given her when he left, dwindled; she became more and more stressed. Her stomach pains became worse in the night. I slept with her and when she groaned I would wake up. She would chant prayers, 'Ramaramarama' endlessly, till the pain became too much. Then she would get up and go to the kitchen. I would feel helpless.

She had two remedies: one was asafoetida and garlic pounded together. If she ate that concoction, she would smell vile beside me afterwards, but her pains would subside. As she got worse, her groans would wake her niece Naani, sleeping in the room next to ours. Naani would go to the kitchen, stir the embers in the fireplace, which she had damped down for the night, boil roasted cumin seed in water and bring the drink to Ammamma. This also would soothe her down till morning.

Eventually, my father's best friend, Nambiar, who lived down the road, put in an application for support to the District Collector. He argued that the income from the two men who had fed a large extended family and kept the house going had disappeared, and the British Government should take responsibility. Ammamma signed in Malayalam script after I had read and translated the letter to her

– she did not understand English.

The Collector however insisted on seeing Ammamma in person, so there was much wailing and brow-beating. She had no cause up to then to deal with officialdom and she was scared, especially as she could not speak or understand English. So she took me along. The Collector asked many questions and insisted on seeing her ration card. I was the little squeak in the middle between the Collector and Ammamma. Surprisingly it worked; we got eighty rupees a month allocated for our survival, and on that we limped through until the men returned and life picked up again.

When the war in Europe ended, no one in our household noticed; the war in Asia was still going on. In any case, we had stopped taking newspapers after my father disappeared; that was the kind of luxury which went first. Along with foolscap writing paper and many of the paraphernalia of education. Schools abolished exams and tests. We had no radio, of course, nor did we have electricity; electricity had not reached our roads. After evening prayer and conjee the house hunkered down quickly, only the washing and cleaning and the clatter of pans providing a backdrop for sleep.

Thalassery life did not change. My father and his compatriots in jail returned slowly, one by one, unnoticed. They quietly slotted back into their pre-war lives, but they had to start their professional lives all over again.

One day, as I was looking out onto the road, a rickshaw stopped and a lanky-looking man unfolded himself. I saw him say something to the rickshaw-man, but the man smiled, picked up the handles and went off. As the person who had got out of the rickshaw collected his suitcase and turned to the house, I jumped up and ran towards him.

'Achaa, Achaa.' I babbled, and hearing me, the rest of the household came to the veranda.

He saw Ammamma. 'Didn't know I was being released until two days ago,' he said, struggling with his bag,

Ammamma's smile stretched from ear to ear and I skipped around Achan like a demented terrier.

'I had no money for the rickshaw,' he said. I was going to ask you for four annas, but he went away. He said he didn't need to be paid.'

My father called Mani to him and gave us both a pat on our heads. I noticed he looked a great deal fairer than when he went; he had also put on a little weight.

It was mid-morning when my father came back for good. Ammamma brought him a cup of tea, the when-in-doubt cup of tea, and the maid carried his suitcase upstairs. In the house, there seemed to be a sense of anti-climax. Now what?

We soon found out.

Ammamma was pleased to hand over the financial reins to whoever was willing to accept it. But, was my father ready, equipped, to take it back?

The day after he came home, we were inundated by visitors -- neighbours, family, friends, party activists, and that carried on for a week or more. He talked to them till he was hoarse and I grudged every moment I couldn't wrap myself around his force-field. As usual, I wanted everybody to go away. Whose father was he anyway?

A few days later the numbers coming to our house petered off quietly. Ammamma breathed a big sigh of relief; she was tired of making tea for so many. Achan spent time in his room, pulling things out of shelves and putting them back. He extracted heavy tomes out of his glass-fronted almirah and looked uncertain. In the second year of his imprisonment, he had requested, and received, permission to have law books sent out to him in the post; those went back on the shelves.

After a little while, he ferreted around his chest of drawers in his room and extracted some sorry-looking clothes. A white shirt and his court-trousers, white, now off-white by being kept on a shelf for two years, detachable wing-collars, and band. Lawyers' clothes. The room smelled of moth-balls and fungus when he was finished. Achan asked Nani Edathy to get his gear washed and starched.

The black lawyers' gown had been rolled up and stuffed into a cotton bag. When it came out into the light of day, you could see how the moths had had a field-day with the garment. It rustled as he shook it out and the whole room smelled of mustiness. He got the maid to hang it out in the sun. Since I would not go away and leave him to get on with his job, he told me to search in the two top drawers of his chest and find his cuff-links and collar-studs. I loved doing little things for him, so this kept me happy for a few minutes. He showed me how to polish his black Bata shoes and this became a labour of love, which I carried out till I left the house for good.

Achan dragged an old dining-table-sized desk to the far corner of the veranda and pushed our rickety bench near it. He got the boy next door to help him move the Dutch almirah downstairs and re-arranged his law books in it. The Criminal Procedure Code took pride of place. One of the two rosewood chairs, the sum total of the seating in the house was placed in front of the table.

Achan then got his old blotting pad out and arranged it on the table. He sat on his chair for a moment, then got up and went upstairs to look at more books.

The next Monday, it seemed my father was ready to go to the Courts. It was only a five-minute walk away anyhow and his best friend, Kunhianandan Nambiar, came to accompany him. Theirs was a story of constant 'accompanying.' In their youth from village to school to college, walking the four miles back and forth daily into town. Then the journey to qualify as lawyers. Subsequently Nambiar's first son was born the same year as I. They seemed to live in tandem. When my father languished in prison, Nambiar kept a benign eye on our family.

I was used to seeing the two men going down our walkway, one curly head, and one porcupine, stand-up hair. One short and a little fat in later years, trundling along with the other, a veritable clothes-horse with the grace of a man used to many sports.

'*Casenthingulum undo*?' (Have you got a brief?) Ammamma asked hopefully from the veranda. '*Illa*,' my father said. There was none. He went anyway to the Courts and returned a little earlier than the four 'o clock when the black gowns normally returned after work; he appeared a little grave.

152

Next morning Nambiar's tout turned up in the morning, when my father was sitting on the steps of the veranda and passing his fingers through his chest-hair, trying to set the world to rights. The tout had two men behind him.

'This is a criminal case,' he said. 'It's your kind of case.' Nambiar specialised in civil disputes. After that, every day for a week or two, touts of other lawyers turned up with clients in tow. My father had a portfolio to work on.

'All the lawyers are out to help me,' my father said to Ammamma.

'The cat needs to jump off the hearth,' she said. 'I'm glad they are helping you.'

After that, there was no holding him back. Now there was a spring in his step, his desk in the corner of the veranda was littered with client-files and law-books, mainly India's Criminal Procedure Code. I was warned off that table, but one day, I sneaked a look at this huge leather-bound tome, he was forever looking at. It was underlined all over the pages in red and blue, and comments were written in the margins. I realised this was the homework he had been doing in prison. Very soon, my father got a reputation for hard work, confidence and results when he represented a client. He prospered.

18

Velyachan, my father's brother, returned from Penang towards the end of 1946. He said that all his savings, amassed over many years working as a doctor in rubber plantations in Malaya, then owned by British men, had been wiped out by the brief Japanese occupation. Only Japanese money was in circulation during that period and by 1946, when the Japs were defeated, it became worthless. In any case, he had not practised as a doctor for three years during the occupation; he and his family hid in their homes, behind closed doors.

Occasionally the Japanese soldiers came marauding, banging at their door. They were notorious for gratuitous violence, specially towards women, so all the women in the house would run and hide in the latrines till they went. The soldiers would take whatever they could find in the house: bread, eggs, fruit, shoes, chickens...

Velyachan hung a big photo of Subhas Chandra Bose, on the wall of his front-room; he was an Indian politician who was aligned with the Japanese, and had pipe-dreams of marching into India with the victorious Japanese army. Bose organised the Indian National Army – he firmly believed that Independence had to be wrested from the British by force. He found Nehru and Gandhi and the rest of the Congress leadership weak in this respect, and left the scene.

Bose was a symptom of the splinter groups that were forming in the Congress; he had contempt for Gandhi's policy of non-violent protest. He was a firebrand who believed that military might had to be fought with sabotage and destruction. He had little or no support within the party. However, within the Congress party, there were sections with different agendas. Mohammad Ali Jinnah was busy with another kind of protest and another portfolio of demands. Gandhi and Nehru tried hard to keep the party together, but it *was* disintegrating.

Bose disappeared and when finally he reached Malaysia he organised the Indian National Army, the I N A, which wore military clothes and marched like an army. He cosied up to the Japanese and expected to mount a victorious assault on India with their help.

The photo of Bose on the living room wall apparently placated the Japanese. Velyachan made a living at this time repairing watches, which had been a hobby of his in peacetime. Later, when he settled down in Ottappalam, his wife's hometown in the South of Kerala, he showed me a clock, for which he had made second, minute and hour hands out of *Irkili*, the spine of coconut palm leaves.

The day Velyachan came back, Mani and I started foraging in her mother's suitcase. What had she brought for us? Many yards of white parachute silk and huge wads of useless new Japanese currency. Mani and I played with the currency and the nylon.

I was too small – or self-absorbed, to realise how emotional Velyamma, Mani's mother, would have been to see her children after six years. It took a

155

week for that to click and then only because I noticed that Velyamma was always keeping Mani close physically, combing her hair, adjusting her dress, putting talcum powder on her face... One day I watched from the doorway as she curled Mani's hair into ringlets using pieces of rags. As I watched, I realised that this was something that had not really come my way. I had no complaints about love or attention but no one had groomed me like this. Mani's mother, whom I also called Velyamma, caught me watching.

'Your hair is thick and too short. I can't do this on your hair.'

Velyamma was kind and intelligent; she had noticed my longing. She was tidy and didn't behave like the women in the house; she talked to my father on equal terms and could speak in English, if needed. She was altogether a different category of female; that was a revelation.

I, however, had begun to have many hair-woes: Alopecia struck around this time, and a bald patch developed at my nape. The only way to hide it was to grow my hair, but Achan firmly believed it should be treated and left exposed to sunlight and air to recover. Many treatments were attempted: first an ointment given by the local doctor, which stung, but it didn't do anything beyond sting. Meanwhile other little bald patches appeared on my scalp.

Another doctor suggested rubbing the spot with half an onion dipped in petrol – this was tried. I went around smelling like a petrol station and in danger of catching fire. I was banned from the kitchen. Then the vaidyan suggested that we soak seashells in lime juice for a week and use the thick emulsion that would form. It stank to glory in the jar and on me. But hair, a few weak strands of it, soon started growing in the bald spots. The Alopecia was quickly forgotten. Petrol and stinking shells, I wonder – how are they related to Alopecia?

After Velyachan had established himself in Malaya in his early youth, in the 1920s, two of his nephews had joined him. If Velyachan, who had run away at the age of nineteen, could acquire a medical degree and become wealthy, surely they would also find their pot of gold there. Madhavan and Balan, sons of my father's sister Dechooty, went there a few years before the war, hoping to make a life, a better living. Many families allowed their sons to go to Ceylon or Malaya in this manner. Today they would be called economic migrants. Madhavan trained to become a nurse and continued to be an army-nurse in India when he returned to live there after the war, but Balan did not do anything. Indeed he did not do anything thereafter either.

Balan came back to India during the war years, well before the war ended. He escaped Malaysia in a Japanese submarine. We heard his version of the story from him, when many months later, he got home, via jail in Madras. I remember him lying back on a rolled-up mattress in the corridor, under the stairs, in our house, with the women of the house dancing attendance.

He was always a good-looking man, but now he was also dressed quite differently from our local mundu-and-shirt staple. For one thing, he was wearing trousers, a rare thing in that town. And, over his shirt, he wore a woollen tank-top. It cannot have been to keep him warm. That tank-top from where I stood, was the hallmark of sophistication, otherness, foreign-returned. He lay back against the mattress beaming; no sign there of the aftermath of his arrest on Madras beach, with his two friends, the subsequent solitary incarceration, the relentless interrogation, or the fact that his two friends had been sent to jail for life, while he escaped by becoming a witness for the prosecution.

All the women listened avidly as he recounted the story of his Japanese submarine adventure. One of the two men who landed on that beach with him on that dark night published a book, long after independence and his release from jail. It was called *Irumbazhikkullil,* (Inside iron bars.) Those who have read this book say it is a bitter indictment of Balettan's role in the incident.

Balettan, however, brought news of the conditions in Malaya, as it was then called, when the Japanese occupied the country. The British had fled, lock, stock and barrel, even the British army had disappeared. But no one was evacuating the non-British subjects – Indians, Ceylonese... Many Indians started walking in the direction of Burma, (Myanmar), hoping to get to India by that route, not unlike the Syrian refugees now, carrying their infants, and whatever else they could carry. On that long and gruelling journey, the Japanese air-force still strafing at them in fly-pasts, the weak died of starvation, exhaustion and Cholera, if they had not been shot down.

Balan claimed he was desperate to return to India and that he joined the Japanese army as a spy for them, because they promised to infiltrate him and two friends of his, also from Kerala, back into India. So, the Japanese army trained them in covert skills, and in the middle of a moonless night, lowered them into a dinghy, on the shores of Madras. They were equipped with bundles of new rupee notes and not much else. The rupee notes were so new and so obviously counterfeit, one wondered whether the Japanese army were at all concerned about their Kerala spies. The spies' instructions had been to bury their dinghy on the beach before travelling inland. As flies to wanton Gods...

All three were apprehended as they dug into the sand on the shore to bury their dinghy; they ended up in solitary confinement, in a Madras jail. Clearly, the Indian police had previous information of their arrival and were waiting for them. What the three men had attempted was treason and they were in danger of being summarily executed. This was a time when Indians were being executed for a great deal less.

19

Ammamma's ulcer did not retreat; she got a little worse each month and by 1946, she was suffering severe stomach pains every night, and some days too. Though it had started when Achan was in jail, it became a chronic addendum to her existence. It also got worse as the months went by; it was as though Ammamma allowed herself the luxury of giving up on herself now that Achan was back.

Eventually, none of her home remedies worked and she called in the doctor. He probed and asked questions and decided she had a 'boil in the stomach.' What was that? Now new bottles of coloured water arrived for her and she dutifully took them, as instructed by Dr Shenoy, the Shenoy who refused the five-rupee note she offered him when he left, who had always rejected the five-rupee notes that were offered during Achamma's illness.

When the cumin water and *Dhanwandaram* Ayurveda pills did not work, she was forced to take to her bed. She would be up in the morning bustling about till Achan went to the Courts; after that she would collapse on to her bed and stay there until dusk. One day, Achan came home from work early and heard her low moan and walked into her room.

'What's wrong?' he asked.

She tried to tell him about the pains, but she was

almost apologetic. Achan sent a messenger for the doctor. When the doctor came he pushed and prodded Ammamma's stomach and gave her sickness a name; it was an ulcer. He prescribed more maroon coloured mixtures for the 'boil' living inside her.

Ammamma took her medicines and stayed in bed. After a month, she became quite weak and could not walk to the bathroom to bathe herself. Naani gave her bed-baths.

Achan started checking on her every day when he returned from work. He usually dumped his gown in front of the door and went in. 'Edayi,' he said (he had always called her Edayi, from the time he was a baby and she, eighteen older had been his 'mother' because Achamma was ill after Achan's birth.)

I followed him in – I always followed him silently when he returned from work. When she didn't answer he sat down on her bed and called her again.

'What happened?' he asked gently.

She opened her eyes and closed them again. He sent for the ever-willing Dr Shenoy, who examined Ammamma again and had a long conversation with Achan afterwards. Achan came out of that conversation looking thoughtful.

After that day, Ammamma went rapidly downhill. I prayed: *Hail Mary's* every evening, and I hedged my bets with 'Ramaramarama' in the mornings. Whenever I found her awake, I sat next to her and told her all about my day – Sister Nympha was angry because I didn't remember the Lord's prayer correctly, something to do with, 'and forgive them their trespasses,' Girija wanted to borrow my necklace again, I got all my sums right... It was

161

pretty desperate – I didn't know what I could do to make her the old Ammamma.

When she started sleeping longer during the day I didn't realise she was slipping away. The doctor came twice a day and my father's face stayed grave when he went into her room.

One evening, when I returned from school and went in to Ammamma, as I did daily, someone had cut all her hair off. It was now an inch long and the grey showed in untidy, lank patches. Clumps of it had been chopped off carelessly and it was as if it had been done with a kitchen knife. I went into the bathroom and wailed. 'Who cut Ammamma's hair?' I asked. Naani took me by my arm and walked me back to the sick-bed. She showed me the lice, myriads of them, tumbling over each other on top of Ammamma's tufts..

I was terrified – there was a custom of cutting long hair into a stub when women were dying and hair was difficult to wash in bed. Short hair could mean that ultimate ending. I fetched a stool and sat at her head, picking lice out. If I picked enough of them out maybe they would let her hair grow again. There were so many I couldn't put them on my thumbnail and squash them. Within minutes, the blood was congealing on my thumb, so I brought a basin of water and started dropping the lice straight into it.

This became a ritual: come home from school, fetch basin, drop lice. Occasionally Ammamma would ask something like, 'Had your tea?' or 'Washed?'

One day Achan saw my vigil; he had also started coming in twice daily, morning and evening. The house clattered on around us, but I was somewhere else, in a bad place. 'Not good,' he said.

When a month had passed, I came home one evening to see a crowd in Ammamma's room. They were murmuring and looking at each other, but Ammamma was unaware. She breathed slowly, with a gasp between breaths. It was terrible to watch and I could not get close to her. I went outside and sat on the parapet beside the kitchen, where my father found me. He sat down, pushed my recalcitrant hair back, away from my eyes, and looked hard at me.

'Is she going to die?' I asked.

'Think so,' he said.

As the darkness closed in, from the corners of that room, where it had lurked during her illness, Ammamma's breathing became laboured and loud, the thing they called tug-of-war breathing in India; I couldn't bear to hear it. So I went upstairs and tried to ignore it. It followed me there into the long night. Achan went up and down the stairs. Lights flared in every room in the house and men gathered outside on the veranda as women congregated in the rooms inside. Neighbours had taken over our house. Dr Shenoy came – and stayed.

As the breathing became loud and hard, I just wanted it to stop. I couldn't think of anything else; it followed me even inside the blanket I pulled over my head. I felt guilty that I wanted her breathing to stop.

When I woke up early in the morning, the house was quiet; I ran down; Ammamma is breathing better, I thought. But she was laid out on the bare floor, as is the custom, with the nilavilakku at head and foot. Her nostrils were plugged with rags. There were quarter anna coins on her closed eyelids and

163

her toes were tied with rags too. A rag was also tied around her jaw to keep the mouth closed. She didn't look like Ammamma at all. I knew there was no one to run our house and look after all of us now.

That shape of death has stayed with me all my life; how could I forget the sight of that woman, who had spent her life looking after other women's children, me included, die in this horrendous manner?

Now there was no one to manage our house. Even at ten years of age, which is what I was at that time, it was crystal clear to me that without another old woman to manage our house, the place would disintegrate. Naani was too young at eighteen years; someone had to step in. During Ammamma's illness, many women of our family came and went. When she died both her sisters were with her.

Ammamma's younger sister Dechooty, had a young family and a husband to look after. She also had the farm and the farm workers to supervise. Naani's mother, however had no such responsibilities; we called her Velyamma as she was my father's eldest sister, a widow at that. Another Velyamma!

I asked her to stay with us, because no one else was doing or saying anything. She was not of the same ilk as Ammamma; she had not lived in town until then, was scatter-brained; I knew she would be a poor substitute. But someone was better than no one.

Achan was not overly fond of her and did not engage her in conversation as he used to do with Ammamma. But a presence was needed and that was what she was. She stayed in our house till the year before her death, at eighty-six years, and as I grew up, I began to realise how clever she was. We had underrated her.

Velyamma tried to do all the things that Ammamma used to do for us, and over the years she got good at it. All she wanted from life was her pan and a little tobacco to chew. My father gave her a monthly allowance for that. She would break off a small piece of dry tobacco leaf and wedge it in the corner of her back-gums. She needed nothing else to keep her happy.

Velyamma wore a mundu and nothing else. No blouse and no top. If there were men around, she would throw a token small towel on her breasts, not really caring what was covered and what was not. Most of that generation of women did not wear tops. The next generation made up for it.

20

When Achan got settled into his practice, life took a turn for the better. For Mani and me, there were more clothes, money for cinemas... Every year, when the rains had stopped and the harvests were in, Bombay Talkies came into town on its annual visit. The large, empty land behind the railway station was levelled and patted down. The travelling theatre would pitch a huge white tent there and advertise their arrival on stickers all over the town. If that was not enough they would send out a bullock cart with stickers on its side. A man inside would proclaim the film to come using a microphone. He would also break into a jingle now and then.

Mani and I would run to the gate to gawp; most of the children on that road would be doing the same. We would pester every eligible male in the extended family, when they visited, sometimes neighbours, to take us to see the three-to-four hour long epic Tamil and Hindi pictures that came to town. They were all black-and-white, but so long as things and people moved on the screen, and burst into dance or song or both at odd, and often inappropriate moments, and made noises, we were happy.

Achan was not a good person to go with; he had no patience and would insist on walking out half-way through the story. If I objected saying I wanted to see how it ended, he would tell me to use my imagination. Sometimes, a wholly unseasonal deluge would come pelting down, pouring in through the gaps in the tent. The sand underfoot would rapidly get soggy with cigarette and beedi butts sticking to our naked feet.

Such a deluge happened the time we were watching the much-lauded *'Ramarajyam,'* basically the story of *Ramayanam*, one of the two main epics of Hindus. Raman, the king-to-be was exiled, so was his wife, Seetha and their children. But his brother, Lakshmanan, insisted that Raman was the king even in exile. So he refused to accept the crown as the next in line, and crowned Raman's wooden clogs as king. Lakshmanan was placing the sandals on the throne with reverence when the skies opened.

In a minute, we were all drenched, as we picked ourselves up and followed the crowd to the exit reluctantly. I wanted to linger, but people were hustling from behind. What happened after that sandal worship? I am still not quite sure.

One of my favourite pastimes was a visit to the beach with Ernest vakil and his daughters, Mabel and Ida. Mabel remained an important part of my life; we met daily, walked to college and to sport events together, and confided in each other. We were both members of the throw-ball and badminton teams. It was a friendship that started at five years, going to Primary school together, and continued walking to College and back when we were in our teens.

Mabel's mother was especially kind to me, when I spent a day in her house; She would cook lentils and rice for me because she knew that was my favourite meal. When I was old enough, she gave me her recipe, which I still use. I keep in touch with Mabel these days on Skype, we complain about the diminishing that comes with age. We gripe about disasters for which there are no remedies.

Earnest Vakil, Mabel's father, had a Maths degree and had studied astronomy. Eventually he had become a lawyer and came to live on Court Road. As we walked home, he would point out the stars and the constellations and talk about dip and declination; with little or no street lighting, the stars twinkled clear and strong and I would get dizzy looking up as I walked. I was the only one remotely interested, though I didn't make much sense of all that either. Many years later I would have to study Astronomy as part of my Maths degree, and Vakil's explanations would come back to me.

In 1946, Mani and Appuettan had gone with their parents to various boarding schools, and would now re-appear only for holidays, until they grew older and took the law into their own hands. They came to Thalassery like homing pigeons when they became old enough to travel alone from school to Thalassery, much to the joy of the household, especially myself.

I once asked them why they didn't stay with their parents in Ottappalam during their school and college holidays. Generally, they would spend a token two days in their parents' home and rush back to Thalassery.

'Thalassery was home. Our parents did not really look after us. They went away for years. Elayachan (younger father, which is what they called Achan) made us feel loved and secure.'

'My father was not a good man like yours,' Mani said to me once, 'though they were brothers. Elayachan cared.'

My father of course cared for far too many people in my selfish opinion, but Mani and Appu were his children as much as I was.

When Mani finished her first two years at College in Trichy she came back to Thalassery and joined my College, Brennen. Again, we looked after each other. Now, in our eighties, both of us, have to do this long-distance caring, which is not quite enough.

In school, I discovered the things I was good at – Maths and words. I got better at sports and did a lot of debating. In short, I was a serious pain-in-the-neck. My father allowed me to grow my hair and I started wearing long *pavadas*. Those pavadas have also disappeared from the scene, the girls preferring knee-length skirts.

These days I watch the slow demise of the sari. Girls wear the *salwar-kameez* outfits, which are more functional. They don't have the grace of the sari, but grace is not a virtue respected in the new, fast-living, aspirational India.

As far as Velyamma, the one who managed our home, was concerned, Mani was perfect; I clearly was not. Mani spent many hours in the kitchen, chopping vegetables, grinding coconuts, doing all the things girls are supposed to know and do. For one thing Achan did not like me – or indeed Mani – spending too much time in the kitchen. He believed that we would fill our heads with gossip.

We liked listening to gossip; Achan had no idea.

169

If he saw me in the kitchen, he would go upstairs and then summon me, to tell me in no uncertain terms that I had no business in the kitchen. To make quite sure, he would give me a job to do – some reading or writing. Mani was strong-willed and he didn't have the heart to make her do things she didn't want to do.

Within the house I got a reputation for being unskilled in all things female. If I ground coconut, the paste was not soft enough and someone else would have to do it all over again. In addition there would be shreds of coconut all around the grinding stone. If I chopped vegetables they were not the right size. I took too long anyway and wasted too much time. I couldn't be trusted to take the pan off the three-stone fire, because I was clumsy and might scald myself. So I wasn't allowed to do much and this too is not conducive to learning.

Velyamma was fond of me and worried about me. She had many conversations with my father in which she stood slightly behind the front door, while he sat on the veranda.

'This child – ' it would start.

This would be repeated several times before Achan took any notice.

'She doesn't know even how to make a cup of tea. A girl can't be like this.

'And she has no obedience in her.'

Achan would call me, and say quite loudly, loud enough for Velyamma to hear.

'Obedience is not a good thing. Especially for girls. No – obedience is not to be promoted.'

Eventually Velyamma gave up.

21

On 15th August, 1947, on the midnight hour, India became independent. The whole household stayed up to listen to Jawaharlal Nehru, standing on the ramparts of Red Fort, Delhi, to make that unforgettable speech about 'our tryst with destiny.'

Now, he said, we were redeeming that promise, a promise made to ourselves long ago. Not completely, he reminded us. We now had a Constituent assembly, which would draft our constitution; the members of that assembly were nominated, not elected. It would be some while before India had its first general election and there was a truly representative government at the Centre and in the states.

Meanwhile a little chunk from the North West of India had been chopped off; another bit had been amputated from the East. The wounds were bleeding, suppurating, and would never quite heal. The surgery was ham-fisted, because the surgeon was in a hurry, and didn't know very much about this kind of surgery.

The man drew lines on a map, bisecting villages, rivers, monuments; in places the line even went through the kitchens of houses. So you cooked in Pakistan and ate in India.

In our elation at becoming independent, we hardly noticed what was happening up north as Muslims

171

and Hindus killed each other by the thousands. The British had left in an unholy hurry abandoning an India they could no longer contain.

My father was chosen to make the Independence Day speech at the big Maidanam, early the next morning, after the Sub-Collector's wife hoisted the Tricolour. She made a short speech in English, which he translated. After that he spoke in Malayalam. There were not many in that town who could slip seamlessly from English to Malayalam and back again.

All the school-children had been led to the big maidanam in town in orderly lines, to participate. We had small tricolours pinned to our blouses and we sang the national anthem after the flag was hoisted. I was so proud, I thought I would burst.

When I became an only child again in 1946, after Mani and Appu left, I started looking for hobbies. Reading was not enough; singing was not an option as it was well-established by the age of thirteen that I couldn't sing to save my life. I had been thrown out of the school choir because I was the harsh note in the front line and I was too small for anywhere else.

I thought dance might be an option. The dance-master was summoned; there was only one in the whole town. He was also the only man who had shoulder- length hair and sashayed as he walked.

After Mani left I had no playmate. Achan, I think, felt a little sorry for my *one-liness*. I capitalised on that. He also arranged piano lessons for me once a week at school and Hindi lessons at home. Anything to keep the brat happy.

I learned to play 'God Save The King' on the

piano and to imitate Big Ben's chimes -- the nun teaching me could not think of anything more appropriate. The lessons petered away when I didn't practise enough, and eventually didn't turn up for lessons.

I learned a little Hindi from my Hindi-master, who was a miserable man, and a little more in school, where it was now a compulsory subject. Hindi was easy to learn and I got decent marks in school exams; I didn't, however, learn to speak anything beyond, 'How are you?' The Hindi master gave up when I refused to sit any exams promoted by the Hindustani board.

Dance, on the other hand, was something I enjoyed. The master came every Thursday because Thursdays were holidays for us Sacred Heart girls. Every Thursday morning, at about ten-thirty, I would start listening out for the sound of him disengaging the latch of the front gate. Dance was considered a sacred art form probably because, like many other Indian art forms, singing, sculpture, instrumental music, it was closely associated with the temple and worship. So Velyamma had to light the sacred lamp every time the master arrived.

The first thing the master taught me was to do a few steps, joining hands to worship the sacred lamp, dancing backwards. It was a beautiful move, lithe and graceful and I always enjoyed starting off in this manner. The first few lessons were simple – getting the rhythms into my head. Since there was no music in the house, Master would use a flat stool and a stick to beat the rhythms. The stick was a foot long and sturdy, while the stool was low like a cutting board. I suspect Naani cut vegetables on it when

Master was not around. Master would sit cross-legged on a rush mat on the floor and get up only when he had to show me a pose or a move.

Velyamma had to stay in the room for the whole lesson, which was about two hours. No way was the dance-master going to be left alone with a young girl of the house, not for a moment. He got ten rupees at the end of the lesson, but the lessons stopped when my periods started. Now I was a 'woman' and different strictures and taboos applied. I could have asked to continue and my father would have agreed, but I started swellings in one knee around that time, and I was forced to rest it. My knees became a chronic issue for a year or two.

Somewhere along the line, the master asked permission to take me with his troupe to a performance in Cunnoor. His star student Seethalakshmi was going to do the *Jethiswaram* dance and he needed a partner for her. My *Jethiswaram* met his demanding standards, so could I go? My father said an absolute 'No.'

'*Jumping about* here is alright, But somewhere else. Mmh.' Velyamma was horrified at the cheek of the master, even asking. I was sorry to see him go, especially as I had never been allowed to perform in public. Much later in life, when I was in my seventies, I would dance a step for my granddaughter, Asha, saying *thathinginathom,* when she was about to go to her nursery. She thought it was wonderful and would laugh happily, until she grew up to the ripe old age of eleven, and reached the '*whatever*' age, when anyone over the age of twenty becomes *not cool* unless they are a celebrity. Now, at eighty-two I threaten to do a dance step in

174

front of her friends if she is cheeky. It works – every time.

22

The bickering within the Congress Party in Thalassery started immediately after Independence. Of course; now there were spoils to scrabble for. One person would represent Thalassery in the new Constituent assembly; who was it going to be? Who would decide? The parties were breaking up along communal lines – Nairs, Thiyyas, Muslims, Christians... I think my father may have been disappointed that he was not selected, though he was clearly the most articulate and self-assured among the possible party members. This, of course, was the Congress Party's decision, having spearheaded the freedom struggle, and the factions in the party had their own agendas.

Thwarted by the party apparatchiks, Achan started planning more personal targets. He finally bought that plot of land he had been looking for, for many years. It was one thousand and five hundred rupees, (approximately £115 according to the exchange rates of that time.) But he had to save for three years before he got there.

It was so near the house where we lived that you could shout to the workmen on the building site from our front-gate -- convenient when it came to moving.

However, the whole building process was fraught – typically, my father had not consulted anyone before putting his money down. They could have told him that there would be problems digging a well or laying a foundation down in what was in fact land reclaimed from paddy fields. Digging that well became everybody's nightmare – the hole in the ground kept getting flooded when it reached waist-deep. The water table was clearly close to the surface; every morning, three to four feet of water would have collected in my father's notional well, so work could not resume till the water was emptied out. Finally Achan had to rent a pump to clear the water just so the workmen could work in there; they had to dig at breakneck speed to the necessary depth before the groundwater seeped up again.

The next step would be to lay down the circular, shaped planks of the gooseberry tree as a lining at the bottom on the perimeter of the hole. The trunk was cut into quarter circles and were a foot wide each and six to eight inches deep. This was for the purpose of purifying the water. Achan held his breath till the planks went in and the sand and gravel to line the bottom, so the well could be left to fill up on its own. I held my breath too as I was old enough to realise that it was his savings, ear-marked for our home, that were being washed away.

The well was the first step in building a house. Then the parapet of the well would come up; after this the workmen could start digging the foundations of the house, knowing that water was on site for them. The foundation, in this case, just would not hold together; it was clear that whatever weight of building you put on that land was bound to tilt and settle, maybe even collapse. So the builders had to dig deeper and the concrete mixture had to be richer, with twice the ratio of cement to sand needed in normal building plots, thus ratcheting up the cost of the building.

This was typical Achan-life. Obstructions and wrong directions taken were the way life happened to him. And when it happened to him, it happened to me too. A roller-coaster ride of highs and lows with us holding fast to each other. Then he would throw himself into fighting the obstacles with fierce determination; when they were overcome, he would glow with content.

Our well, in the decades after, turned out to be the only well in the neighbourhood, which always had crystal-clear water right through the summers, when most wells in the neighbourhood dried up. On any day we would have the maids from three or four houses coming to our well to collect water.

Surprisingly, my life too has taken every wrong fork in the road it could possibly find, I've had to fight all sorts of imaginary windmills, and at the end, I would always feel a sense of accomplishment, and live on for a few months until the next life-cyclone hit me.

But, for both of us, there was an important but: paddy fields surrounded that plot on three sides. In terms of a view, the place was idyllic, as I was to find out when I reached that time when I wanted to sit alone and dream. In the far corner away from the house my father set up a seating area made up of broken concrete blocks and bricks. When his friends came visiting, it was there he sat. And when he was not around of an evening, I took my current book there, reading and contemplating the vast fields around, listening to the beasties in the fields, and focusing on the silences around me

178

We moved to our new home in May of the year I started College, -- 1950. Achan had named the house *Anand Bhavan* after me – Anand's home; which was also the name of the Nehru family home. The Thalassery wags nicknamed my father the local Nehru because he wore a Gandhi-cap, shaped like a paper-boat, and a waistcoat like the one Nehru always sported. No one else in Thalassery wore a dark brown, wool waistcoat, exactly the shape of the garment Nehru wore over his long jubba. According to the hoi-polloi, who determined the opinions of Thalassery, I was his Indira. And, of course, my mother, like Kamala Nehru, had died of tuberculosis in her daughter's childhood.

When our new home was finished, I could see that it made no concessions to the womenfolk who might live there. My father's quarters upstairs were entirely separate from that of the downstairs dwellers. The staircase to go upstairs was on the veranda, so that he could come and go without reference to anyone else. As usual, I floated between the two floors.

On moving day, we had little to do – no moving vans or packaging. We had so little by way of worldly goods, we picked them up and moved them by carrying them across to the new house. All I had was my clothes, which fit into one cloth bag, and a handful of books. I would start College in a few months' time and happily discarded my old exercise books. I dumped the rest in the back of my father's newly acquired Austin, Standard 8.

Achan put his law books in his car and the neighbours carried the few items of furniture on their shoulders. I picked up my cat on the way out; she continued to walk back and forth every day and pestered the new occupants of our old home, establishing squatters' rights in their kitchen. Eventually she gave up on them when she realised there were no children there to give her sanctuary under the folds of their sari.

Upstairs, in my new home, was a balcony, with a parapet around three sides of it. Wooden railings made the parapet secure, so that no one could fall out. Sitting on that red cement parapet, Achan would drink coffee and talk politics with his friends. I began to see the point of the all-bachelor layout of the house: Achan and his friends could keep up as late as they wanted and make a great deal of noise in inconclusive political discussions without disturbing the quiet life of the women downstairs.

The floor of Achan's balcony room was painted in the colours of the Indian flag, though the orange was more maroon than orange. But, full marks for effort. Later in life, he became disillusioned with the corruption and cronyism within the Congress Party and the Congress Government and eventually he left the party. He continued to work in local politics, mainly in the Town Council, promoting diversity. He supported the first Muslim who became the Chairman of the Thalassery Municipal Council.

Of the two bedrooms upstairs, one was earmarked for me. The house was full of windows and my room had four windows on three walls; Achan had planned for a house flooded with light and air. Two of my windows looked out on the main road and the buses hurtling past were noisy during the day. Then as now, the bulb-shaped horns on the vehicles were loud and frequent and I got used to that. Early in the night, the buses and cars would cease and the night would be quiet. Then I could hear the laughter and the conversation from Vasu's little shop across the road; it was a friendly accompaniment to my reading.

The bit that made me uneasy was the music used at festivals from the large Muslim house across the road. The women of the household were good friends of ours and we visited each other now and then. However, occasionally, there would be a ceremony, and a special keening music. The one that made me sleepless was that of circumcision, which had a background riff of clashing knives. It generally started late at night and would go on for weeks every evening. For that period, once or twice a year, I would shut the windows facing the road firmly, to keep that noise out.

I spent my college years in that house, Anand Bhavan, and my attitudes to caste, religion, life and death slowly crystallised. I read frenetically. In college I was doing Sciences, but my interests were veering towards History, Political thought and Economics. Political thought, in particular became a passion of mine, and has remained so to this day. I started reading Sabine, Catlin, Russell and Laski – heady stuff for a seventeen-year-old. Mukerjee et al's Indian History was long, printed on bad paper in small print, and I found it boring. Nehru's *Discovery of India* was a great deal more interesting. I waded through Churchill's war books, enjoying the rhythms of his prose.

I discovered Trevelyan and Ketelbey and became

181

familiar with British History and Chinese History. In the early fifties I had trouble finding books about the Chinese dynasties. Books about the enclosures of land in medieval England were also rare, until I chanced upon Tanner.

I spent seven years in that house till I got married and went to Ceylon. The monsoons came and went, rice in the fields surrounding three sides of my home grew from paddy-green turning to golden yellow, as it matured and dried on the stalks. In the swampy fields, my house-boy, Prabakharan, caught fish for our supper, when the fish-man didn't turn up. The water in the paddy-fields looked pink rather than muddy-brown, and the frogs set up a choir every evening. I read Lin-Yutang and immersed myself in the sounds and sights of that peaceful place, listening out for the crickets as they buzzed me to sleep.

When the harvest was done, the fields would begin to dry. Soon it would become hard turf with sharp paddy-twigs sticking out of them; you couldn't walk on them with any ease, especially barefoot. Then the ground would be damped down, three or four men digging the bristles out, flattening the soil, and beating down with heavy pallets. Two bamboo poles would be set up on the field, a thick rope tied across, and young men would play badminton and volleyball. Some years there might be a tattered tennis net doing duty if the lawyers up the road donated their previous year's net. That side of the house would wake up with the sound of men calling to each other and the thump of racquet on rubber; it was something to watch in between turning the pages of my books.

At fifteen years of age life was throwing up a lot of propositions. However, the next significant question mark in my life was the sari. In normal Thalassery households wearing a sari is not a big deal. Our neighbours were mainly lower middle-class people and some of them wore saris daily, as a matter of course. But, in my house, nobody ever wore a sari. The women wore the traditional Malayalee costume, the *mundu-veshti*: a white sarong-like cloth with a similar cloth on top draped over the shoulder. So, where was I, at age fourteen going to learn how to drape six yards of material around me.

In my class of forty girls, six or seven had graduated to saris; these were generally girls slightly older than the rest. They had mothers or sisters at home who owned and wore saris daily. These girls had done their practising over full-length mirrors (another thing we never possessed), and done their tripping and falling on the lintels at home.

I was the youngest girl in my class, courtesy of my cousin registering me at school when I was just four. Saris were not even in my remote sights when, suddenly, the girls of my class decided to have a sari day on which all of us wore saris. Where from? I didn't own one. How? But I dutifully pestered my father for the regulation two days and he marched me off to P A Chettiar's textiles shop, after I convinced him this wasn't a joke.

I chose a white nylon with huge pink lilies on it. Not a great choice for a novice as I was soon to find out. The print was more upholstery than clothes but I didn't notice; the material was soft and slippery. Achan had been reading a newspaper while I did my choosing, which had become his habit whenever he took me clothes-shopping, about twice a year. He generally paid without looking, as he had become prosperous by then, his practice expanding beyond his wildest dreams. I was pleased with myself.

From next door, Madhavi taught me the basics of sari-wear. I practised gathering the pleats carefully and dropped the whole bunch of pleats down to the floor several times. 'This material is too slippery,' she declared. She brought a voile sari of hers and I found that easier.

When the day arrived, the nylon sari would not cooperate. As I pleated the front, it kept collapsing in a slithery heap. When time ran out I found several safety pins and tucked the sari into my under-skirt and pinned it in many places.

When I thought the sari and I had come to a truce I went to find my father, to show him his 'all-growed-up' daughter. I shall never forget the look on his face. Disbelief is the closest word I can use to describe his state.   Shock was another one. He looked almost sad. As I went to school I was not sure the recalcitrant sari would hold up – it had a will of its own. And I was remembering my father's face.

Did I outgrow my father in some manner at around fourteen years of age? My many puppy-loves were clearly not something I could discuss with Achan. In the spring of that year, a young man came to our house to sit his (S-S-L-C) Secondary School Leaving Certificate exams. He was the son of a relative and went to school in his village, where there was no exam centre – he had to sit at the St Joseph's Boys' School in Thalassery. He came with a cloth-bag of books and a change of clothes. Ammamma gave him a *jamakkalam*, a thin cotton quilt, a *pulpayi* (grass mat) and a pillow without a pillow-case. He slept on one end of the veranda; early in the mornings, I would see him moving his books around as I left for school.

I saw his face only when Velyamma served him dinner on the floor, on a tin-plate, in front of my study-desk. Velyamma would sit near him and enquire about his family and his village; she seemed to know all of them. That is the only time he came indoors.

This boy was fair and had beautiful eyes with long lashes. He never said anything much, so Velyamma had to do all the talking when she served him his food. He ate alone, quickly shovelling the food into his mouth. I was flushed and excited, he was so handsome; I would lift the flap of my desk and hide behind it till his meal was over, afraid my face would give me away. After the exams he went away. Bala-something-or-other. He was an incipient doctor, I found out later.

There were several Balas after that. So many names in Kerala start with Bala: Balakrishnan (which is what my husband was called), Balanarayanan (I knew two of those, Balagangadharan, Balasubramanyam ... I fell for one boy after another: a just-gowned lawyer; a police officer who dazzled in his khaki shorts and his arrogance, a commandant, he called himself, and a young man who played tennis on the District Court premises. We, Mabel, Ida, and I, took a shortcut every day through the court premises walking home from school, and later, college. The young lawyer's

185

forehand ended up in the nets when I walked by and I was pleased.

The Commandant came and went – he had briefs to discuss with my father, who was Public Prosecutor. If my father was away when he came, he would stand in the yard below our front veranda and leave detailed instructions in English about what he had come about. I gathered he liked keeping me talking and I'm sure he figured that the feeling was mutual.

Girls were not supposed to talk to young men or even '*throw eyes*' at them – Velyamma's derogatory term for sneaking a look. So I wasn't going to confide in her. My father protected me from all male predators by not allowing them access. Men were not permitted into the female areas of the house unless they were very close family. Inside the house was a male-less world. I would be quite embarrassed to discuss my fantasies with Achan. Here was another place where my father was totally useless. Our worlds were beginning to expand and drift wordlessly apart, and I was beginning to have dreams that he had nothing to do with.

In college there were little liaison's springing up and dying natural deaths when courses were completed and students transferred to other colleges. I did not fancy any of the young men in the courses I took, though some of them were friendly, almost. One of my friends down our road told me the boys in our year were a little scared of me. I was perhaps too young at sixteen to take any of them seriously, and in terms of maturity, they were way behind all of us girls in that year.

Some of the girls who were well and truly hooked lived surrounded by a miasma of longing and self-doubt. I often spent lunch-breaks with a friend of mine who, like me, read books; we generally sat on the thin strip of grass behind the Biology lab, where we thought no one would find us. Sometimes a girl would come looking for me there and unburden herself; there was obviously an obsessive need to talk about the non-relationship.

I have always suffered this kind of unwanted outpouring, with women wanting to share their emotional problems with me. The girls showed me long love-letters and expected me to read all nine pages of them and offer support. Some of the letters were smudged in part, the words difficult to decipher. Tears? And I was totally without any wisdom in this department. All I did was listen and that seemed to have been enough. Did they come to me because they knew I wouldn't gossip about them? Looking back, my only virtue was that I was totally non-judgemental.

Any budding relationship was conducted in clandestine fashion. If families knew, they would be angry and aggressive, perhaps stop the girl going through college, get her married to someone else. One of the girls I knew committed suicide by swallowing copper sulphate when her affair was discovered; such was the ignominy attached to having any kind of emotional attachment, which was not sanctioned by the family. All she had done was write a letter that had fallen into the wrong hands.

There was so much going on around me in my college years that Maths, which was my main subject, became incidental. For some unknown reason, Maths came easy for me right from Primary School, and enticed me into its rigorous premise. If English was offered as a main subject, the choice would have been easy. English, however, was only offered as a side-dish, a subsidiary subject. I had too many helpings of that side-dish, indeed I gorged myself on that, and had no space in myself for the main dish I had opted for. This degree in Maths was one of those wrong turnings I took in my life; it determined so much of my future. However, in 1974, when I came to England, it was that Maths that made me a worthwhile person for a school to employ, and led to my life here – such was the shortage of Secondary Maths teachers that year.

I neglected Maths and went on a reading spree. The library in Government Brennen College was a well-kept secret. I discovered its riches almost by chance and dug deep. I read through the shelves without discrimination. My two library cards were not enough; I borrowed others from girls who never went to the library.

I was the bane of the Librarian. I could see his face screwing up in a frown when he saw me approaching down the aisle. It was hard work. I would walk down the aisles just to look at the spines, pick two at random, and go to the librarian's desk. I wasn't supposed to go to the library to borrow books more than once a week, but he couldn't turn me away when I presented all the other cards that I had begged or borrowed.

Soon, the librarian decided he might as well give in to this girl breezing through his books. I was thrilled the first time he called me to his desk. There were piles of new books of many sizes, shapes and colours on his crowded desk and he was trying to catalogue them.

'These are new books. I haven't listed them – can I trust you to bring them back soon if I give you a few?' I think he knew the 'soon' as not an issue.

So we had a negotiated understanding. The lecturers in the English department also noticed my book-greed. Two of them started giving me books that they had personally ordered for the library. I was well-catered for.

I neglected Maths at college, skipped lectures, didn't keep notes and didn't listen to Mr Manickavajakam, our ponderous Head of Maths, who taught us Calculus between two and four of a Wednesday afternoon. Ponderous and immediately soporific after a lunch brought daily from home by our 'boy.' I blame those lunches for my undoing: predictably, rice, a vegetable curry and fried fish. Delicious! Calculus didn't stand a chance after that.

We were only five girls in a class of forty Maths pupils. Girls sat in the front and got on with their work. Generally. One day I nodded off while the lecturer was talking about Differential Equations. The textbook in my lap dropped to the ground with a thud. Rema, sitting next to me gasped. Manickavajakam was livid.

'You, girl. Anandavalli, 'Stand up.'

I had to stay standing for the rest of the two hours. The lecturer hated me thereafter.

A week later my father called me upstairs when he returned from the Cosmopolitan Club.

'I met that teacher of yours.' He said. 'Short man. Fair.' I knew what was coming.

189

'He says you are going to fail your Maths.'

'Won't fail,' I said. 'Won't get a good pass though.'

'Well, you see,' my father continued. 'I sent you to college; you wanted to go. And sitting at home doing nothing is boring. I thought college would keep you occupied. And – if you pick up something on the way, going and coming, that's fine. I shouldn't worry about exams.'

I could have hugged him. 'I missed some lessons, and I slept in his class.' I confessed.

'He told me. And, that man is a bore,' he added

I would have been much happier studying English Literature or Politics and History. But that fork in the road where I chose wrong, led to a life as a Maths teacher in Secondary Schools and as a Maths Adviser for the British Council's overseas projects. This does not mean I disliked Maths, ever -- how can I hate a discipline of such great structural beauty? But there were other areas of knowledge I might have been happier studying and working in. In recent years Paul Auster (in 4 3 2 1, short-listed for the Booker Prize of 2017), and before this, Penelope Lively, in more than one of her books, have written about the choices we make, which determine the rest of our lives, when we are not even aware how important the choices would be.

23

My final years at college, 1952-1954, were also the years when a slow murmur began to surface about my getting married. It came from die-hard, older members of the family as well as friends. Nambiar, one of my father's best friends, whom he saw on a daily basis, would volunteer casual comments. Nambiar always walked around with his *mundu* lifted up slightly, and one finger discreetly scratching his arse. I hated his throw-away comments; he had several daughters, why didn't he go away and get all of *them* married?

'Girl's getting big – time you started looking for a husband for her.'

Achan consistently ignored the comments, though they embarrassed me. And then there were elderly uncles and distant cousins who picked up the refrain. Until my father straightened up his slender back one day and looked at the offending person.

'She is going to study. As long as she wants. And she is not getting married till she is at least twenty-five.' *Hip Hip Hurray*! After that all the elders shut up. For a few years.

Meanwhile I discarded the *pavadas* (long skirts) and blouses of my school days and graduated to saris. In the first year of college there was not a single girl who didn't make concessions to the fact that we were now in a mixed school. The ratio of boys to girls was approximately five to one then. The girls, all thirty or so of us, crowded together in the seats in front, and the boys gathered behind, in the long lecture halls, some ready for mischief.

I had just turned fifteen during the summer holidays but had shot up and a sari didn't seem a joke anymore. Father accompanied me to the *Chettiar's* shop again and I got six saris and six blouses – my lot for the year. I had no idea of matching and colours, so I picked the six lengths of cotton for blouses merely *because* I liked the look of them. Girls with efficient back-up at home, such as mothers and elder sisters, knew how to wear the right garments together, blouses carefully colour-coordinated with saris. It took me another year or two before I learned to make the most of my clothes. Shopping for the sake of browsing in shops and looking at things you never intended to buy was never a pastime then; in the little towns in Kerala it still isn't.

The girls had their own common room and the rest of the college was the territory of the boys – under the trees, in the lee of out-buildings, on the verandas -- a kind of unspoken segregation. We didn't communicate with them and by and large they left us alone. There was one boy, I remember, who had a reputation for groping and we called him spider – he of the eight limbs. We always made sure that we did not stand or sit in front of him on the city-bus. All of us girls knew the boys and men we had to be wary of, the ones whose hands behaved without any reference to their heads. In joint-family existence, girls like Mani and I had to watch out; we would alert each other if we sniffed a predator; they had a distinct smell, an amalgam of lust and guilt.

Meanwhile, even in Thalassery things were changing: city buses started running in Thalassery early in the fifties; there was a stop in front of our house and another a five-minute walk away, near the Civil Courts. It cost only four annas to get from home to college. So the rickshaw-men and the jutka-men lost their jobs and they have become almost extinct in Thalassery. Almost, but not quite. Until that last horse dies and that last rickshaw collapses in a heap of old wood, canvas cloth and hopelessness.

My rickshaw was pulled by a quiet and caring man called Usman. Some of the time there was another waster called Krishnan, who often came to the job drunk. Once he dropped the handlebars while I was in it; I fell back face-up and was scared of the rickshaw for a few days. He also consistently lied to my father about me delaying the pick-up from school, when in fact it was he who had turned up late. So when Usman became our rickshaw man I was pleased. He always came on time, did not stop at the toddy shop on the way back from school, ever, and was invariably reliable.

However he started a painful dry cough in the second year of our acquaintance. It was chronic – it got better in the dry season, but when the rains set in, he would have to put the rickshaw down periodically to catch his breath. When I told Achan he spoke to Usman. Usman said he could not afford to stop pulling his rickshaw. Achan thought Usman had tuberculosis; it was a common disease, especially among the poor, at that time (late forties) and I lost sight of him after the bus-service arrived.

Surprisingly, many years later, when the number of rickshaws had died down to about five, in the old bus-stand, where the rickshaws congregated, I often saw Usman sitting in front of his rickshaw. There wasn't much work. The rickshaw had become old and tattered like him – tears in the rexine of the seat, handle-bars rough from wear. He would smile happily and greet me and ask about my family.

He had survived and It was always a pleasant surprise to see him.

Now of course, there are auto-rickshaws, *phut-phuts* as foreigners call them, motorised and noisy. They are a cheap substitute for a taxi and they park in the same bus stand, now renovated, where the rickshaws used to pick up the passengers who got off the buses.

Moving from one home to another down the road seems to have been a sudden growing-up event for me. Or was it the fact that I was now in college, in a mixed institution moreover, where I had to learn some new realities. There, for the first time, I found many new ideas floating around, which I had not heard so openly discussed before: marriage, love, boys, work... A group of us would sit in the girls' small dining room and discuss matters of great import (according to us). Nothing was taboo. Sometimes we got so wound up in our arguments that I forgot to reach my 2 p m lectures – with dire consequences.

That group, my peers, are almost all gone now. My favourite of the lot, Lakshmi, died two years ago. How engaged, indeed animated, we used to get, talking about something as juvenile as the buses in Madras with their advertisements on their sides.

194

Where did they go? And what did we decide about extra-marital affairs? And what was our conclusion about free love?

College was also the place where I began to feel I might be able to write. A compulsion to put words down on paper was taking hold of me. This was inevitable because of all the words I had amassed reading for so many years and with such desperate speed.

As part of the degree course we had to study examples of prose. Our set prose book was a collection of essays by Ruskin, Hazlitt, Lamb, Stevenson... And a long treatise on the American War of Independence by Edmund Burke. I devoured the writing with a sense of glorious discovery – I can do this, I can, I kept telling myself, while I read those masters again and again. I wrote my first essay in that year,1953, titled, *The Educated Unemployed*; it was published in the College Magazine. The job market in Kerala had not kept pace with the numbers coming out of the new colleges that proliferated after Independence, and only the well-connected were finding jobs.

The next year, I wrote again for the magazine, this time about the works of Aldous Huxley, especially *Time Must Have A Stop*. I knew then, as I know now, that this kind of essay writing is what I do best. However there are no men or women of the calibre of Lamb and Hazlitt writing essays now-a-days; has this art form died a natural death? Now, late in life, I write blogs instead; they have the additional advantage that they can be short, they are *my* perspectives on matters, and I don't need to please the gatekeepers of the writing world – the agents and publishers.

Once upon a time, the University of Madras, to which Brennen College was affiliated, insisted on everyone doing Compulsory English (Part 1) and a second language (Part 2), either Malayalam, Hindi or French, as well as our chosen speciality (Part 3), in the first two years, which was then known as Intermediate. In my case the speciality was Physics, Maths and Chemistry. Equal weight was given to all the parts and you had to pass all of them to proceed to the final two years of an Arts (!) degree.

Students now-a-days have no such luck. They can go through college and acquire amazing degrees without ever gaining any fluency in English. One would imagine this in itself is not a great loss; people in Europe get by on their own languages without having to learn English. The problem is that English remains the one language in which all of India can communicate with each other. For this reason, perhaps, in spite of aggressive advocacy from the North, Hindi has never acquired the status of the national language.

The real problem used to be an inherited one; India spoke many languages, but Malayalam and all other local languages were discouraged in many schools. Instead the better schools stuck firmly to English as the medium of instruction. Malayalam, at the time of Independence did not possess a vocabulary to learn and teach sciences. But as the years passed, Malayalam has grown, budded and flowered. Now it can discuss Science or any abstraction with ease – the vocabulary has grown into the space age, to meet the demand. When I travel to Kerala these days, I am catching up; I am entranced.

At school, after Independence, we had to learn Hindi, but it was not examined and I did not proceed with it afterwards. Malayalam of course became the medium of instruction in Kerala. That lasted for a few years, but job interviews were conducted in English all over India, and the language of the work place was English. So private schools reverted to English. Now, students passing out of them seem to have a huge advantage over those educated in Malayalam. In the globalised arena of multinational companies and a proliferation of tech companies, English rules.

I now regret the fact that I didn't learn enough Hindi to get by, because it is an easy language to learn; it is also the language closest to Sanskrit, the language in which India's epics, *Ramayanam* and *Mahabaratham* are written. Furthermore. I can read and write and speak a little Hindi now, but not enough to get by in the North, and when I am in the north of India, I do need this language.

The South insists that the infliction of Hindi on it as the language of administration on a regular basis would handicap them. It would be a great disadvantage with jobs and entrance to courses because they would find it difficult, for many years, to compete with Northerners on a level playing field.

Language battles are fought in India with great rancour, as they are in Northern Ireland, Sri Lanka or the Catalan region. The present Modi government, fiercely nationalist as it is, is trying to make Hindi India's language at the United Nations. Many Indians would not understand the subtleties of the U.N debates if they were carried out in Hindi. So there would be a quite novel situation in which part of the Indian delegation would be in the dark about what was being said by the Indian representative.

24

I feel that I spent only a short time in our new at home in the Konor paddy fields, but in fact I spent seven years in that house, till I got married and went to Ceylon. However the idyllic existence in the *konor* paddy fields was suddenly and severely disrupted when the first national elections for India were announced. From 1947, until the general elections of 1951, India managed with a Constituent Assembly. In those four years a new constitution was drafted, as always with noble sentiments – equality under the law for all Indians irrespective of caste, creed or religion... It is a moot point whether those ambitious ideas were ever adhered to; in the time of Narendra Modi as Prime Minister, no one is even pretending to do so.

There were the exhilarating five-year plans, major infrastructure projects and good will to all neighbours. Young men and women like me felt motivated by the rhetoric; we assumed action would follow. There was non-alignment and the slogan *India Cheena bhai bhai (India and China are brethren)*, there was hope. Some of these dreams were realised; others fell by the wayside. Certainly, the standard of living for the working classes have improved vastly; their expectations are high and they are realising a great many of them.

In 1951-1952, My father stood for election as a

candidate for the Legislative Assembly of the state – we were still in *the Madras Presidency* at that time as the States Reorganisation was yet to happen, and our Legislative assembly sat in Madras. By 1951, it was eminently clear that the Congress Party in Kerala was losing ground to the Left, though it was doing well in many other states.

The local party machinery organised itself, meetings were called, speeches made; my father did not have time to breathe. With all that, even *I* knew the chances of the Congress Party winning the seat in Thalassery were nil. A part of the Congress Party had split away from Congress and formed the *Janatha* Party; for the election they threw their weight in with the Communist Party of Kerala. The Janatha party was a hybrid in itself constructed out of remnants of the Congress party, which had split away, and the Socialist Party, which was not making too much headway in the Thalassery area.

People were disgruntled at the unfairness prevalent in society, where a few rich landowners treated their workers with casual disregard. The Communist Party had a local newspaper called *Deshabimani (National Pride)* and its message was clear – this society is uncaring of its workers and must be dealt with.

In its favour, the Communist party's organisation could not be faulted. The small cells of party activists in every village and locality, met with people, not only at election time, but right through the year. Across from my house was a corner shop; on its veranda a group of workers rolled *beedies*, from tobacco leaf left over from exports and local manufacture of cigarettes. The dry leaf was delivered in gunny bags and the beedi workers sat on the floor in the shop, while *Deshabimani* was read to them. The workers were paid according to the number they rolled each day; the man who read their newspaper was paid a day's wage too.

Many years later, in the elections of 1998 – 1999, I remember a group of carpenters doing some woodwork for me in my garage in Kochi. I would be sitting on my veranda idling, Malayalam newspaper in hand, and listening to them discussing their voting options. They were impressive in their knowledge and passion for politics. No wonder Kerala has huge turnouts at elections.

The methods of the Communists were many: murder, violence practised by the Naxalite wing, as well as enthusiastic canvassing in the villages and towns. I went canvassing for my father with a group of Congress activists; it was clear to me that he was going to lose. But no one was telling him that. Did he know?

For the period of the election my house was a Congress hotel as well as a party office. Naani cooked huge pots of rice and when they finished, she cooked another pot. I would often come home from college to find the rice in the pot was eaten and she was hurriedly cooking again for us. There were men staying overnight, men whispering in corners, men planning and conspiring. My father was out of the house daily speaking at meetings around the constituency.

On election day, I was a representative at the polling booth; I had a list of the voters in front of me and would tick off the names as they voted and left. I would also check that the indelible purple ink had been put on the voters' thumbs. This would not clean off for more than twenty-four hours.

When the votes were counted, the congress party and my father had been comprehensively defeated. He found it difficult to grasp why the people of his town had rejected him in favour of a Johnny-come-lately Communist. Achan went to bed and did not come out of his room for a day-and-a-half. He used his bedside bell to summon tea or coffee while the victors rejoiced on the roads. They made it a point to come in bus loads, stop in front of our house for inappropriate lengths of time, and shout victory slogans. Next day, his close friends dropped in cautiously to sit with him.

In terms of ideology, I was in favour of many of the reforms the coalition was suggesting, but the communists in the coalition had been killing people rather than relying on the democratic process. They were admirers of Stalin's dictatorship in Russia (some unfortunate boys born at that time were named Stalin.) and had no constructive ideas about how to redeem the working poor in Kerala.

Kerala had woken to the fact of the age-old oppression of the tenant by the landlord, and the worker by the owner of the business; It was long overdue. In Kerala wealth needed to be redistributed; trade unions needed to get more effective; tenancy laws needed revision. The new coalition could at least try.

25

I got married in 1957; many years later, I have wondered why I consented to get married at all. This is a question many young Indian women ask themselves, and have been asked by foreigners, who just cannot comprehend why a self-assured, well-educated young Indian woman would consent to an arranged marriage; it seems so contrary to their personality. There is one remarkable congruence in the answers of many such women – they had to get out. I too had to get out.

I told Velyamma one day, only half in joke, when I was twenty years old and she was moaning about my unmarried state.

'I don't want to be married, but I want twelve children.' I didn't think being married was a prerequisite for having children; I was also trying to outrage her.

She jammed her fists into her ears, saying, 'I don't want to hear this,' and disappeared in disgust.

When the proposals started coming, my father said that I could veto any man I didn't like – and I did exercise this veto many times. But I could not go out there and browse, make my own mistakes. There was no fun attached to this arranged process; it was more like choosing a car than choosing a husband. And I would have no second-hand value at all.

I lived in a cage; the cage was without doubt

gilded, and the inside of the cage was filled with love. One has to be a middle-class, small-town woman of Kerala to understand the nature of our incarceration. For all my father's forward-looking ideas, as I grew up his certainties began to crumble. They didn't crumble as a function of time or my age; it was his bewilderment at the phenomenon he had to deal with, me!

I was not allowed to go anywhere on my own. This is normal; this is the case with all families, who consider themselves 'respectable.' A maid would accompany me if no relative was available. There were two places I was allowed to go on my own; one was to the house of my friend, Mabel, which was a five-minute walk away. My father also made an exception and allowed me to go to the local beach, the small maidanam, where I enjoyed sitting on the jutting rocks and watching the fanfare of the sun going down, the slow, orderly pink-and-orange descent, and at the end, the sudden inglorious dip.

I did a great deal of my thinking on the edge of the promontory at the southern end of the *maidanam*. Though there were concrete benches to sit on, scattered around the beach, they were foul – the families who lived on the slopes above the beach who had no latrines would come to the maidanam to defecate. So there was excrement in various stages of disintegration in front of the seats.

In my corner at the far edge, with only rocks below me, I was sublimely alone. Here I did all my thinking. I thought about music, men, books and all else. I decided that I could not be bothered with rich clothes and jewels in an India, which was fundamentally poor. I went through a phase when I wore only simple white clothes and put my gold chain away. Achan did not interfere – 'White? OK. White it shall be,' he said.

My girlfriends got fed up of what they called my posturing. And certainly there was an element of posturing in this abrogation of coloured clothes and gold chains. The bit my friends hated most was the fact that I refused to accompany them to the regular Sunday afternoon matinees at Mukund Theatre, which showed three-hour-long Tamil Films. I was refusing to join in into what they thought of as group-activities.

I think my father started worrying when a few men began taking an interest in his precious daughter. He could not fathom how far the interest went or how I may have reacted. A lecturer at the College where I was doing my degree started writing letters to me. Some junior lawyers expressed an interest in marrying the vakil's daughter. It was all very low key, but people were beginning to notice this strange girl: bookish, confident, with opinions of her own.

And then I met a young man, a crazy young man, and realised we were two of a kind. He spoke my language, made me laugh, and for a short two months, he wooed me. He sent me books, telegrams, and long letters, sometimes two a day when he had to go back to his job. I thought he would come back, but he dumped me, not even very gently. He confirmed my view that, when all was said and done, I was not attractive to men. All my life I've nurtured that inferiority, like a bald patch or a chronic rash.

In my angst, I asked my male cousins:

'What's it with me? You guys are all chasing so

205

many girls in the family.

'I am fair. I have got nice hair. So -- ?'

One of the cheeky men amongst my cousins said, 'See that wall over there, Anandam. It's white. Do you consider that attractive?'

I gave up.

My father probably thought that when his precious daughter decided to get married, there would be a long queue of eligible young men in front of our house. He may have been a little flummoxed when the crowds didn't turn up. It didn't help that when the odd young man did come along, the horoscope wouldn't match; my horoscope was so awkward that I did not take proposals seriously till the kaniyan had been and gone. People around me could see Achan's uncertainty and inexperience.

The elders in the family now reminded him that it was his fault – bringing up a young girl without due regard for convention. They smelled blood – and pounced. They began pestering my father, warning him of all kinds of disasters if I was not reined in, '*cabin'd cribbed, confined.*' I swatted away the first few proposals, which came to me via my maternal grandmother. But the old men and women were like a well-choreographed dance-group. They came, dispersed, re-gathered and sashayed back.

On the part of my harassed father, here was definitely an abrogation of responsibility, strange for a man who had held so tight to his role of father. He let the buzzing crowd of old men and women take over the process.

Now the proposals multiplied. Without exception they were young local lawyers. I rejected all of them

– if I was getting married, I wanted to get out of that small, claustrophobic town, far from the chaperoned excursions into the living world, far from any place where everyone knew everyone else. Marrying a local lawyer would mean I had to spent the rest of my life in that town. I knew Thalassery was a small part of the world; I wanted my share of the rest of it.

In 1953, I had represented my college at a debating competition in Madras. I travelled with a college mate of mine, also a debater. We stayed at the Women's Christian College and had a chance to see how the urban young lived. We travelled around on the Madras buses with Ovaltine advertised on the sides, ate at restaurants on Mount Road where the Biriyani was amazing, and had an experience of freedom – going where we wished, planning our excursions and making friends with the Sri Lankan and Madrassi girls who lived in the College dormitory. I was hooked; I wanted this freedom. I wanted to wander and see all the places I had read about, preferably alone.

The other major factor in all my decisions then as now, has been the insights I gained with my inveterate reading. That world out there, a very large and wonderfully diverse one, was beckoning. John Gunther's *Inside Africa,* for instance, made me realise how circumscribed my world had been; I needed to be out there to claim my share of that world. Recently, with the Brexit issue raging, and many nations wanting to shrink into their limited nationalist identities, I am surprised we want to settle for less rather than more. This world, all of it, is the birth right of human beings and all other living beings. At eighty-two, I am greedy for all of it.

In the United Kingdom I wanted to see how *Westminister* worked, the places where Fabians met, and the British Museum. In addition there was Holmes's house in Baker Street, however imaginary, Madame Tussauds, The Tower of London and Buckingham Palace. In those days you could go right up to the door of No 10 and get photographed with the security guard. I reached all those places – and more – and the wonder still stays with me in 2017, in spite of the rough sleepers, the filth left uncollected on the streets, the dog turd and all else. I visited, finally, on my way home from Nigeria, in 1962.

How can you beat a place, which includes Kew Gardens for instance? And the Planetarium. To this date, just about mobile now, senility setting in, and having to ration my excitements, when the train from Croydon draws into Victoria, I feel the buzz. Nothing to beat London, I think, and am immediately energised.

If I travel from Purley to London Bridge there is the Millenium bridge. Raghu, my son, who was a Structural Engineer, specialising in bridges, did some work on it. He would point out that bridge to me because he knew I claimed ownership. He was there on the bridge the day the queen opened it and the security guards asked him to stand aside. When it started wobbling, I called him 'My expert on wobbly bridges.'

I also had a date with Africa, which I fulfilled in 1962, starting from Nigeria. I spent twenty-five years of my adult life in education in Africa, in Sierra Leone, Nigeria, Uganda, Zambia, Kenya and Malawi – I was very lucky. To dream and to live my dreams was humbling, especially as I realised how little we,

208

the West, or Asia for that matter, could offer Africa, and how much they could teach us about being human.

In Africa, I was never an expatriate – I was 'Mama'; and they let me into their homes and hearts in many countries. In Kampala, mine was the only dog that barked at *Mzungus*, (white people) never at Ugandans. My counterpart, David Nyakairu, would stand at my gate and call out,' Is that dog going to bite?' and I'd answer, 'Are you white? He will bite if you are white.'

The dogs in expatriate houses were trained to bark at black men because it was black men who broke into *Mzungu* homes and ran away with radios, television sets, music systems, computers, clothes, shoes... I was comprehensively burgled in three countries: in Sierra Leone, the burglars broke in, sat in my sitting room and drank through my liquor cabinet, collected the clothes from the linen cupboard and wash basket and left nothing behind. On the way out they hoovered up my electronic gadgets. The next day I had no clothes to wear to work, so I got some material from the market and got a dress made overnight. Fortunately they left my malt (Glennevis) behind as they did not recognise the name as alcohol.

There were armed guards at the gate in Sierra Leone as I was living inside the British diplomatic compound, which had high security fences and blazing lights, but the burglars were not deterred. In Uganda they took my television and my watches and pens. And when I left they kept back two containers, which were scheduled for my next post. In my home in Lilongwe they left nothing behind, except the furniture.

All our display of wealth and possessions must have been irksome to some Africans who had nothing. They were very few of that type of African around; most Africans lived in fear of those predators too. My colleagues had to come to my house sometimes to work together on reports and plans, so I taught my dog not to bark at them

As the months slipped by, the attack from the elders of my family about my unmarried state became two-pronged. My grandmother warned me:

'Your father is ageing prematurely. He is looking tired. You will send him to an early grave worrying about you.' It was an organised and well-considered attempt.

Others kept scaring my father about 'scandals.'
It didn't help that I suffered from a serious handicap – I was not only 'educated,' that was bad enough, I was a graduate and had a reputation for too much reading. I was full of words and was a debater of some merit. Most of the men in Thalassery had a fear of women more educated than them. In the Nair community, from which my father had to find a husband for me, the educated men were mostly lawyers. Some were junior lawyers who worked with my father and I had seen them come and go. Most would never make a living at law; they would live off their ancestral land.

I realised I had to get married if I was ever going to see the world outside Thalassery. I couldn't stay in that little backwater of a town, doing nothing but reading, no opportunities for working, going anywhere, meeting any young men. I took stock of my circumstances and said to my grandmother, 'I will accept the next proposal that comes my way. So long as he has two eyes, a nose, and all the other bits and pieces.'

The next one that came along was my eventual husband. What a way to make a decision!

Balan, my husband for two decades, was educated, worked as a civil engineer in Colombo, and sounded harmless. As far as my family was concerned, he ticked all the right boxes. He was thirteen years older than me and I have never, to this day, quite grown up. It was a recipe for disaster. But -- get me out of here, I thought, and that was that.

The bridegroom and his family normally come to inspect the bride before a decision is made about the marriage: her looks, the financial status of the family, the house, and her level of education; This practice continues to this day. I remember one instance when a prospective mother-in-law asked me to walk in front of her, to check me out. I got my own back: when she asked me my age, I said thirty, when I was in fact twenty-two years old; my cousin who was trying to arrange the match was disgusted with me.

As usual, before the day I got married, I had seen my husband-to-be just once, when he came with his sister, for the *pennu* (girl) *kanal* (viewing), the seeing ceremony. For sheer awkwardness, you could not have conceived of a better procedure. Kamala, my sister-in-law to be, had style and grace and tried hard to ease the awkwardness of the pantomime of my *pennu kanal.*

Brother and sister travelled from Colombo to

211

Madras for this event, and I understand they stopped off in Trichy on the way to see another possible bride. Like buying a house. When they came, Kamala also picked up a college-mate of hers from Madras for moral support.

The masked dance called *pennu kanal* took place in Madras, (the Chennai of today) in my uncle's flat. My father did not meet my-husband-to-be till the wedding. Big mistake, as both Balan and I discovered, gradually, when all the excuses on his and my behalf, had been exhausted by both of us, and there were no places left to hide. It was not his fault, of course, that the wife given to him on a platter did not adhere to the general profile of a young Malayalee girl in 1957. I was simply not good marriage material. It is hard to know which of the two of us came out worse from that ill-conceived pairing.

It was also not his fault that he was a confirmed Colombo man and I was, in every respect, too other for him. He didn't speak Malayalam and found my family difficult to talk to. They all tried – his family, my family. Kamala, Balan's sister, was the person who master-minded the marriage; she made a gargantuan effort to reel me into the new world, their world.

After this one non-encounter called the *pennukanal*, the next time I saw my brand new, just unpacked husband would be for a few minutes at the wedding ceremony, and afterwards, in the bedroom, nuptial bed covered in embroidered, purple, slippery, satin sheets and sprinkled with rose petals. The memory still makes me want to scream; the petals in particular.

212

26

In the weeks before the wedding, I was carried along on the flow of the preparations. There were clothes to get together, necklaces and bangles to be chosen, many sessions with the local tailor to get the sari-blouses sewn in time. He was established with his pedal Singer machine on the edge of a veranda shop, within calling distance from my home.

The wedding was a night ceremony like most Nair weddings in long-ago days, though recently they have become day-time events. The house was bursting with family and friends; every room you walked into there were richly attired women; the compound was humming with men, busy getting the *panthal,* made of bamboo and coconut thatch up, and supervising the cooks' lists. My father's favourite nephew, Keshavan, was in charge; he had a gift of making all life into a joke; he saved me from looking fully at the massive life-change coming.

On the afternoon of the wedding, I had a serious attack of the jitters. As usual, Mani came to my rescue.

'They're all downstairs. Come upstairs with me,' she said. 'let's go to your father's room.'

I gathered up my wedding sari, a Banares off-white silk, with a rich gold border, my gold brocade blouse, underwear and a towel. My hair was still dripping wet from my bath only a few minutes before. Upstairs was mercifully empty; we bolted the door and I started getting dressed for the event.

I stripped and got my home-made knickers and rowka (home-made bodice) on.

'Don't you have a bra?' Mani asked, looking at me as she often looked – with thinly concealed exasperation at my lack of feminine skills. Today, in our eighties, I come across that look still.

I had never owned a ready-made garment of any ilk up to that day. She ran downstairs and came up with one of her new Maidenform bras. When I put it on, even I could see it did surprising things to my figure. Mmm.

I passed a comb through my wet hair to get rid of the knots. It was still dripping. Mani seized my small towel and wiped the ends off impatiently.

'Leave a few knots,' she instructed. It will keep the *konda* tight and bulk it up.'

Mani plaited my hair in two hip-length plaits and wound them, first one, and then the second one around it, on the back of my head. She then decorated the hair-do with pieces of jasmine garland.

People knocked and shouted at us to open the door. Women in the family would want to see the bride being dressed – Mani had helped me escape that ordeal. Dressing the bride is normally a communal affair – family and friends have a right to watch; we were denying them this little show.

Make-up for me was a token dusting of *Cuticura* talcum powder on my nose, a large magenta *pottu* in the middle of my forehead, and *kohl* on the inside, bottom rim of the eye, applied with a forefinger. How quick and easy was that?

Today, there is a professional hairdresser and make-up artist to dress the middle-class bride before she is smothered in gold. Gold is bought by the kilogram by middle class parents.

The only mirror we had was my father's small round shaving mirror; so I had a good look in it; I seemed no different from usual. A little pale perhaps, but It would have to do. I wound the sari around me and secured it with a nappy-pin at the waist. The gold on the sari made my face glow. Mani tugged at the bottom. 'You are not walking in a puddle to lift the sari so high,' she muttered.

As Mani and I were finishing up there were frantic knocks on the door. We didn't respond. The someone knocking at the door repeatedly was not giving up. 'Open,' my father called out. 'I need to get into my chest-of-drawers.'

We opened the door and Achan came in.

'Locking me out of my own room...' he murmured. He unlocked the top drawer of the chest-of-drawers, and took out my new gold necklaces, just three, not the bust-covering jangle of today, and my six bangles. He looked stressed.

'Better get these on,' he said. He gave me a long hard look. 'You alright?'

Daft question. I was in zombie land and did not answer.

As he went down the stairs the *Nadaswaram*, the closest to a trumpet in traditional south Indian music, started its jaunty statement of celebration, the music of the Gods, from the far corner of the compound, loud enough for the whole neighbourhood to be alerted; the drums came on joyfully to accompany it. Now I was petrified; the rhythm of that music was

215

insistent; no getting away from its message.

A flame flared up in my stomach and subsided. I sat down on my father's bed waiting for my nerves to settle. When I went downstairs, I knew I would be on show. The family of the bridegroom were coming, one by one, and I had to accept greetings and gifts and respond to pointless conversation with strangers. And smile till my jaws ached.

When I had calmed down, I decided to go down and meet the mob; my cousin, Naani, as usual was looking out for me. She was at the bottom of the stairs, and as she saw me coming down the stairs, in my bridal sari; she looked right and left and grabbed my hand.

'You look as if you've seen a ghost,' she said. She took me, sleep-walking, to the kitchen. 'Chance to get some coffee,' Naani said. This was her carrying out her life-long job of feeding me, caring for me, wiping my tears. After that quick gulp of coffee laced with love, I walked back to the sitting room, past the back veranda. In the right-hand corner of the back-compound, there was furious activity, a little furtive.

There was a whole subculture being nurtured there. Keshavan was busy giving directions to the cooks and when he was busy there would usually be mischief. I noticed that, in between talking to the cooks, he was quietly fiddling with a carton full of something. I stopped and looked. Then the something clanged, and all was revealed. My cousin was secreting several bottles behind the washing-stone, where our maid generally beat our clothes to death. I didn't have to ask what they were.

216

Liquor was not meant to be served at Nair weddings, but there would be a steady demand from a few men who could not enjoy anywhere or anything unless propped up by Arrack or Gin. As the night grew darker there would be a steady stream of devotees slipping away from the front of the house to the back, almost led by their noses, the poor, addicted sods. These were the same men whose livers would, in Keshavan's picturesque telling, drop off in the vicinity of the Cosmopolitan Club.

The kitchen had been empty except for coffee and tea in huge urns. All the rest would be cooked in huge *urulis*, wok-shaped brass and aluminium pans, outside, by Brahmin men. They had set up several three-stone fires and the flames under them were rising high. Two of the men were dealing with enormous quantities of rice: they were spreading cooked rice on pristine grass mats, a layer of hot, steaming rice, then a raw layer, then again a cooked layer – the raw rice would cook in the heat and moisture of the rice above and below it. Rice is always slightly under-cooked at wedding feasts by design; apparently it slows down the process of rice getting spoilt.

Nair husbands were traditionally men of the night. By custom, Nair husbands never lived with their wives – they just came in the evening after dinner from their own homes, and left their *methiyadis* (wooden clogs) at the front door, slept with the bride and departed early in the morning. Apart from procreation the men were obliged to give their wives a measure of coconut oil, salt and cloth every year. Marriages would have sat lightly on both husband

217

and wife; the husband did not even own his children then, though this has changed since.

If the wives got bored with the men they took the men's methiyadis and left them outside, a warning not to come in. The children were fed and clothed and educated by the uncles. The women often had several partners, though not at the same time, and it was well-known that the Nairs were a polyandrous society. Except, the uncles decided when and with who. Still, I felt I was born too late!

My husband lived in Ceylon, so this was going to be the end of Thalassery for me; this was also the end of being just my father's daughter.

The urban, educated professionals in India, these days, find their own partners and respect no caste rules. Thank God! The women are able to do this because of financial independence. But, most of India lives in villages and continues to respect the dictates of caste and religion. I cannot imagine this will change any time soon, but it will, gradually, as parents and community give in to their young, and as more women get educated and take their fate into their own hands. Fortunately, families in India are totally committed nowadays to the education of boys and girls; they will sell their ancestral land to see their children through school and college. They dedicate time as well; if you travel early in the morning on a commuter train, you will see mothers and fathers helping children with their homework.

In passing, I should mention that this devotion to education can be carried too far sometimes. Children as young as five are interviewed by certain schools for entrance, exams start at Primary level and the pressure on children to perform, to succeed, is extreme. On the other side of the coin, children are not resistant to education and discipline is not a major problem in classrooms in Kerala as it can be here in England. I should know; I taught Secondary school for ten years in this country and I still carry the scars.

Too much education, more than the man, would have been a serious handicap for girls in the fifties. But not any longer, because young men now, want a second earner in the family, especially if they live in America or The United Kingdom.

.

In old Nair weddings, you got married in the night, the new husband spends the night at the bride's house and departs very early in the morning, with his male friends. There wouldn't be any female friends because only male friends are allowed to accompany him to his wedding ceremony.

In the morning only a maid, carrying her suitcase (and an umbrella – de rigueur at this point) travels with the bride to the new in-laws' place. There they will be feted with tea and sweet-meats before the maid returns. The bride too will return after a day or two. All of this has changed now and men and women participate equally in the various stages of the marriage; Indeed my husband's siblings and wives turned up for my wedding.

The Kaniyan decreed that there was no auspicious time for me to leave my home, for another two days after the wedding, so, I could cut my tail off in stages. My husband, on the other hand, was straining at the leash. He could not understand anything but the most basic Malayalam, he didn't know how to wear a *Mundu* (He got by in a Ceylonese sarong, which was worn only by Muslims in Kerala.) He was not comfortable in our home.

Family and friends streamed in to see Raghavan Nair's precious daughter's new husband. Balan volunteered a strained smile and didn't say much. The local people didn't feel comfortable in English and my father struggled to observe the niceties of Malayalee discourse, translating for son-in-law and friends.

Two days later, I left by the early morning train to Madras, Sad to say, I never gave leaving my father a thought, until the moment came when I had to pick up my bags and follow a stranger out my front door. I doubt my father had realised the nature of this parting either. When I went up to say goodbye, he was standing in the dark, staring out at the fields. I stood next to him for a moment and stared out too, Then we both cried, until my father's brother came up in search of me and scolded my father.

'It is inauspicious to cry like this when she is going to her husband's home. Let her go with your blessings.'

On our way to Madras to board the plane to Ceylon, we had to stop off at Ottappalam and Palghat, where family insisted on welcoming us. After lunch and tea at Mani's mother's house in Ottappalam, we drove to Palghat to my cousin's house, where another feast awaited us. It was eleven in the night and food was not on my agenda. I missed my father and wondered when I would see him next.

At twelve I was wilting, but my cousin was in good cheer. I was relieved when I heard a car outside braking to a stop; tomorrow's transport to the station, fourteen miles away, to Olavakkode Junction, I thought.

It was my precious father come to find me again. Keshavan had felt sorry for him and brought him all the way from Thalassery for another quick goodbye. What joy it was to see him again! It no longer felt like a big goodbye – just a small one.

'I'm warning you, it's too easy to come to Colombo,' Keshavan said to me. 'Easier than driving here. He'll be pestering you, you wait and see.' Keshavan had a gift of making things right when they were threatening to go wrong; he could never bear to see me or my father sad.

I had mercifully little to take with me – a medium-sized leather suitcase, my first ever suitcase, donated by my uncle Damu, who had a habit, still does at ninety, of knowing exactly what I need. In that suitcase were my few saris and jewels, my one pair of slippers – plastic, see through -- and not a single book. A strange aberration for me, but books had always found me whenever I needed one, so I was sanguine. I had this mental image of books, big and small, trite and profound, Malayalam and English, forming a neat line and following me.

I was excited about my first plane journey, all of one-and-a-half hours to the domestic airport of Colombo with the lovely sounding name, Ratmalana. There would be a short stop at Jaffna in the North of Ceylon. (Jaffna, of course, later, after the eighties, became a place to which the Sinhalese did not travel. And the Tamils who lived in Jaffna would be unwelcome down South -- unwelcome as in killed.)

Balan's family was used to this journey as his parents travelled frequently to their home in Alathur, near Palghat and his sisters went to College in Madras. His brothers, one elder and one younger, had both married Kerala women and this too was a strong link.

I was told that I had to keep my luggage below forty-four pounds and if I was personally too heavy, I might have to leave some of my luggage behind. Balan did not, by nature, communicate much and I couldn't really get any answers out of him. He kept saying, 'Depends on your luggage.' So, when I queued up to be weighed and issued with boarding cards, I was concerned. I was not exactly fat, but neither was I petite. The husband standing behind me in the queue was a stranger and not much help.

My first piece of good luck was the man in front of me in the queue – he was huge. If he could get on, I could. And yes, they weighed every passenger. At the end of that little panic of mine in the queue, I wondered what my new husband thought his association with me would entail. You couldn't call it any kind of relationship – yet.

Balan had great virtues that I didn't comprehend at that time. I was on my way to Colombo, a new, bewildered bride. I failed to know, and he omitted to tell me that there would be a welcoming posse' at the other end, who would scrutinise my face, my clothes, my jewellery, my talk, my walk. He didn't know or care about appearances – this was one of Balan's strengths. So I didn't 'dress up' for the journey. One doesn't dress up and wear gold necklaces for travelling. However I fished out my one pair of sandals from my suitcase, and slipped them on for the journey.

The posse' was small. There were two bouquets, which I could have done without, already burdened as I was with hand-luggage . Kamala, Balan's sister, represented the new family; there were two or three others I didn't quite register. However, I did notice Balan's three bachelor friends, because as soon as he saw them he abandoned me to the rest of the welcoming party and went off to talk to them.

The three, Weera, Freda, and M.G he called them, smiled shyly. They were his friends from Ceylon Technical College, where they had all prepared for the degree in Civil Engineering. They were much darker than the usual Kerala Indian, I remember thinking.

I would spend several evenings with that trio at Saracens Club, the sports club in Colombo, which had not then made any concessions to women like me. No drinks served but beer and ginger ale. A toilet fit for purgatory. And no women came to that club ever, when I was there in the evenings. I got the message, and after two months, I stopped going; Balan went back to being a bachelor, and went alone to spend his liquid evenings with his schoolboy friends. They were really nice young men, and later, whenever I met them, they looked out for me; they stayed friends.

When I disembarked at Ratmalana airport I could see Kamala had brought her pomp with her -- Cadillac and liveried driver. This now defunct domestic airport is nine miles from Colombo and is no longer an international terminal. We travelled in style to the family home, which was empty, as Balan's parents were in India at the time.

I kicked off my sandals and looked at the house as I got in – huge rooms and empty spaces. Magnificent pink floors -- the deep pink of Cardinal polish -- staircase fit for the dramatic descent of a princess. I went upstairs, found a bathroom and washed my face. As I did the royal descent, I noticed the noise level had increased downstairs and there were a few more people, all smiley faces. I could do that; I smiled.

Some more were wandering in and out. A Tamil resident maid called Pakkiyam made tea and coffee. As I reached the last few steps of the staircase, a tall man turned up, in a slate-grey suit. 'My husband, Nadesan, ' Kamala introduced. I looked at him, slipped the remaining steps and landed on my rump. He was outrageously good looking. I was mortified but everyone pretended they had not noticed. I literally lost my balance, stunned by the looks of this man: chiselled features, a smile to go on a Kolynos toothpaste advertisement and the height to set it all off. He stayed a moment, didn't sit down and went away saying, 'I'll see you in the evening,' flashing that quick smile. There was an inbuilt air of arrogance about him; later, I would learn that he never came to his wife's home; indeed he never came in my time there. So he was just showing elementary courtesy to a new bride.

'You are coming to our house for dinner,' Kamala said. I had nothing to say, so sat and watched and listened. They teased Balan, but it all went past him. Thankfully they left soon. I went to bed and slept for a long, long time, waking up only in time to go for

224

dinner.

Kamala's house was a treasure trove, full of beautiful things. Chinese screens that I was scared to go near, Persian carpets on the polished deep pink floors, and flowers everywhere. This was another world and I had no idea places like this existed except in films. I remember the Anthuriums, red, white and pink in every corner of the veranda. And the roses, huge vases full of them in every room.

Kamala's friends, Mona and Khoban turned up, full of laughter and friendliness. 'We came to see the bride,' they said. 'Let's look at you,' said Mona, and later, 'You have to come to our house soon.' They filled the house with happy ordinariness and I found I had things to ask them and say to them. I got my words back, those words I had spirited away from so many places, and tucked away in my heart, while I sat on the little promontory in Thalassery's small *maidanam*, and watched the breakers eating into the land. For as long as I lived in Ceylon I loved that couple. They toned down the excesses in my sister-in-law's house and made me feel less an outsider.

27

After that eventful first day in Colombo, I knew I was in alien land. Tiny mind that I had, it focussed on that deep, shiny pink of the floors in the two houses I had been to. We had similar concrete floors in Thalassery, but they never had this gleam. I watched Pakkiyam do the floor in our house that week. They had a different type of broom, one which was more like a brush, mounted on a long handle. The brush was made of husk and shaped like a triangle. Much more efficient than the short brooms in Thalassery, which killed Maathu's back. Now, when I am in Kerala, I ask for Sri Lanka brooms and hey presto, some of the supermarkets produce them. After sweeping, Pakkiyam had to get down on her hands and knees to polish the floor once a fortnight.

Pakkiyam was short, surly and round; she rolled rather than walked. How did she manage to cook, serve, wash clothes by hand, iron, clean the huge house and keep her temper? Well, she *didn't* keep her temper. She was a second generation Tamil immigrant, who had been loaned to my husband's family until she got married. When she realised that I was not in the habit of ironing clothes – I just folded them up and wore them – she was contemptuous.

How could I explain my rather limited clothes culture to her? In Thalassery, we did not own an electric iron. We had an old coal iron, which was not safe to use because the handle was loose and the iron was liable to open and shed coal all over the clothes on a bad day – and it had a few bad days in my hands. Then again you had to burn dry coconut shells to produce coal and fill up the iron every half an hour or so as you ironed.

In the end, in our Thalassery home, no one cared much about clothes. You bathed in the mornings before school or work, and this meant washing your hair daily as well, had two oil-baths a week; clothes were washed, starched and folded. Sometimes they were starched so mercilessly that they could possibly get up and walk. This was just our house; many girls in college wore beautifully ironed clothes. With us the only clothes that got regularly ironed were my father's white, long-sleeved shirts for the Courts, his trousers, which again he wore only to the Courts and his wing-collar and bands.

I remember a week into my arrival in Colombo, Pakkiyam came upstairs to ask me whether I needed anything ironed. When I said, no, she was clearly bemused.

'The other *podi nona* (young madam – she was referring to another daughter-in-law of the house.) always has her saris ironed,' she informed me. I fell another step or two in her regard.

Whenever I contemplated the house that we lived in in Colombo, I had a sense of pointless space. Two of the three bedrooms upstairs were huge. I did a reconnaissance – looked out of windows, opened empty cupboards and let the cockroaches escape, smelled mould and futility. There was only one window that had a decent view – it looked out on a beautiful garden and manicured lawns. So I dragged our double bed into that empty room and transferred our clothes into the room-sized wardrobe, which contained very little. Balan's parents never came upstairs, so I could do what I wanted with all that space. I doubt Balan noticed he was in a different bedroom now – that was one of the nice things about him. He was happy to 'go with the flow.'

I still had nothing to do – there was only so much you could do at a window. Balan came back from work at five-thirty, had tea, and went out after a bath. First he did his filial duty of taking his father for his evening constitutional at Galle Face beach. After that he would go to Saracens for the evening and return around ten, smelling of Becks beer and Benson and Hedges. I didn't mind the smell of cigarettes as I had grown up with it, but the yeasty smell of beer was another matter. In Balan's outings I was perfectly welcome to go with him, but it was not important to him. Gradually I stopped accompanying him to either place. My father visited three months later to check up on where I had landed and was aghast that I stayed at home while my new husband spent the evening out.

Meanwhile, I was searching the rooms for any trace of anyone reading anything. When I mentioned it to Balan, he started bringing a newspaper home – the Times of Ceylon – which Nadesan would edit some years later. I read every page, all of it, including the advertisements. Like starving people eating wild roots and berries. Balan's mother noticed my frenzy of searching for reading matter.

'There's an old almirah in the loft upstairs,' she said, kindly. 'You might find something there.' And

Kamala said, 'You're supposed to be on your honeymoon. What's with you and books?' I didn't have the heart to say that I hadn't noticed the moon or the honey.

I found the loft and the old Dutch almirah with the panes broken. Silverfish, I could see, were having a banquet, and shreds of yellowing paper dropped out as I opened any book. There were a few, still in readable condition, if I was willing to ignore the debris on and around it. I salvaged three of them and carried them down to my room like a trophy -- a translation of Bhagavad Gita, and two more in the same vein: semi philosophical. They would do for a few days. I should have taken some books with me from India, I knew then, but even if I considered it, how would I have taken them with the luggage on the plane?

I had heard many of my friends who had arranged marriages say that they fell in love with their husbands soon after the wedding. I waited. There was nothing objectionable about Balan; we just lived in different adjacent bubbles.

Much later, years later, I remember thinking that it was only an Indian arranged marriage that could randomly throw two such, quite harmless, but totally incompatible people, such as me and Balan together. And yet, there are many comfortable, if not happy marriages too. Or are their expectations in some cases too low? Then again, in the West, are expectations too high, causing breakdowns? If I had a choice, looking back, I would still prefer to make my own mistakes and take the consequences.

Colombo had been a revelation – I had never seen such a clean town anywhere in India. No debris floating around on the streets, no smelly sewers, no rubbish hillocks. There were no open latrines in Colombo – the sewage system worked and the indoor toilets were pristine. Every middle-class home had more than one bathroom and the maids made certain that they were clean.

I was learning quite a lot quickly. Within a few weeks I knew a little more about putting an outfit together (if I had one, that is). I knew how to bring that gleam to the floor: (you applied the Cardinal polish with a rag painstakingly by hand, then you wrapped a big old towel and determination round a brush and brushed the floor to perdition. When red polish stopped coming off on the cloth, or on your feet, you applied colourless Mansion polish and did all of it all over again. The floors ended up stunning. If you put a splash of water on it, it could even be lethal.

Two months into my marriage my in-laws and I were getting the measure of each other. I was learning things about myself and about them – things I would not have dreamt of in Thalassery. Some of it was disturbing. I learned that my husband's family, for some obscure reason, expected my father to shower gifts and money on the new son-in-law. They were clearly disappointed. I could see that the family was conferring about something they considered important, and it was to do with me.

They often retired to the father's room, where I would never dream of going, when one of Balan's siblings came visiting, and whispered. When they came out of that conclave, they hinted. I let the muttering pass, but there was no escaping the gist of it. Finally it came out in the open when the big brother, a doctor, turned up for a holiday. About thirty-five thousand rupees was the sum touted around. And did I have brilliants in my jewel box? That too was expected. All the Nair women wore brilliants.

When it got really insistent, I decided I had to come clean.

'You made a mistake, I think,' I said. 'Did you imagine I come from a wealthy family? Not so...'

In retrospect their mistake was quite amusing.

'But your father is the leading criminal lawyer in the town and you are an only child.'

'True, but even if he had money to give you --,'

'Yes.' They were eager for my response.

'You can have money, or me – not both,' I said. I continued, 'As for brilliants, what are they?' I had only two pairs of earrings anyway: they both cost thirty rupees each and I knew they were not precious stones. One was a gift from my uncle, Balan – I cherished it because he really couldn't afford even that.

I thought all white stones looked alike. Thankfully, they gave up on me.

My brother-in-law, the man of the family, a self-assumed role, never forgave me. '

'You think you are a goddess,' he said.

Balan thought it was a huge joke; he really didn't care. He was a good man in many ways and probably didn't deserve an odd-bod like me.

My expectations about marriage were pathetically minute: get out of Thalassery, stop my father

231

worrying about me, have children – lots of them.

My father came on a check-up visit around Christmas 1957. We were both in a conspiracy to reassure the other. He noticed that I did not go on the evening drives when Balan took his parents to the Galle face beach. It was a daily routine established over many months when Balan had slept on the dining room table to reassure his mother he was within call. His father was weak, old and doddering and his mother needed Balan near.

I would sit on the terrace upstairs with my father when the family was out.

'You don't go to the beach?' my father asked. He knew how fond I was of sitting by the small maidanam at home.

'I like being on my own,' I said. I didn't tell him that when I sat at the back of Balan's Austin quietly watching the beach, I was dreaming of a small beach on Court Road, where I had a spent a lifetime of thinking and putting words to my imaginations.

I could see he was a little uneasy about the situation.

'A man who doesn't love his mother will have no love for his wife,' he said; he could have been reassuring himself.

Since it was Christmas around the corner, my father and I went out together and bought gifts for the children of the family: books and diaries and key-chains. He insisted on getting a copy of Nehru's *Discovery of India*, for Baba, Kamala's stepson.

Knowing Baba as well as I did I tried to dissuade my father, but he insisted. Kamala smiled when she saw the book; she knew that book would never be opened, let alone read. Baba was a stunning young man of fourteen years at that time and his very good looks were going to destroy him. He grew more and more feckless as he got older, took to alcohol in a big way, experimented with whatever came his way and died early, in his thirties. With all that, we were friends, that boy and I, and his death was a horrible waste of a young life.

Nadesan, Kamala's husband, who always kept a judicious distance from his in-laws, took a liking to my father and would send his car almost every evening to pick us up; it amused my mother-in-law. Nadesan loved talking politics – Ceylonese as well as Indian – with my father. My mother-in-law whispered that Nadesan missed the company of intelligent men and my father was interesting. Interesting? That was one way of describing his febrile mind.

Achan noticed the level of waste in the house. Colombo 7, the posh, rich enclave of Colombo, which included Colpetty, where my sister-in-law lived, and Bullers Road, where I lived, had a casual relationship with money – the kind where you didn't have to think about it very often. I had come from a home in which no waste was countenanced; when Naani prepared potatoes, she didn't peel the skin off, she scraped them.

One day, we were at Kamala's for lunch and the *Cokie* (cook) decided to sweep the dining area just before serving lunch. I got up from my chair to let him sweep and watched the debris as it went. With paper and dust, a half-loaf of bread was being swept away; in my house in Thalassery bread had been a rare luxury.

In Thalassery we bought a small quarter loaf

233

when we had guests and we wanted to make a quick accompaniment to tea. The dosha skillet would be rubbed with ghee and sugared slices of bread would be toasted on it. When Mani came for holidays, she would occasionally ask for bread. Otherwise we had no use for bread. As the bread preceded the broad end of the broom down the corridor to the kitchen, my father and I looked at each other in astonishment. I decided to find out why this was happening.

Cokie was a Tamil migrant who had come many years before to work in the tea plantations and eventually ended up in Colombo as so many like him did. He was an exceptionally inspired cook. I didn't know Tamil, but I had picked up a little Sinhalese in the three months I had been there. Sinhalese has many words, which are similar to Hindi and I could stumble around in that language if had to. I still carry this little bit of inadequate Sinhalese in my head.

Cokie had fish on the hob, which he was cooking for the household help – there were more of them than the family. The fish floated in a rich orange-red sauce, which made my mouth water just looking at it. Cokie discerned my greed and let me taste the fish curry – it was superb. So he put some in a little bowl for me to take to the table. The table already had chicken curry and Biriyani, fried mutton and vegetables. I kept my fish near me and protected it by eating it very quickly – this was the first time I tasted home-cooked fish in Colombo, which could match Naani's fish curry at home.

Cokie did a little deal with me when no one was looking. Could my father send a little money, eight hundred rupees, to his family in India? He would pay me in Ceylon currency. Exchange control restrictions had become more rigorous with the years; apparently he went home to India only once in three years, when he had been able to save enough money to make the trip worthwhile. This was like the Kerala men who go the 'gelf' for years at a time, and return loaded with *Halwa,* Nido milk powder, dried fruit and yearning for family, and that baby that had been born in their absence, and was now two years old.

Having noticed the easy waste in Kamala's house, I made myself comfortable in my high moral ground and wondered whether Balan was similarly wasteful. He never went shopping; the tailor made up six cream-coloured pairs of trousers every year I was told, and he bought ten identical white shirts and that was that. His mother ordered vests and made him underwear from white cotton cloth. I kept a safe distance from all this.

Some evenings Kamala's brood would turn up and cajole Balan to get jujubes for them. The shops were a five-minute walk away, but he would take the car out late at night to indulge the children. My father's car in Thalassery was used only for emergencies; I walked to college, he walked to the Courts and the car sat in the garage. It belonged to the neighbourhood in that if there was any emergency, such as illness, weddings or late-night journeys, the families on our road would borrow our car and our driver. Eventually Achan sold the car because he could not afford the fuel for this neighbourhood use.

'Since Raghavan Nair bought a car, nobody on this road can use their two legs to walk,' my Velyamma used to mutter.

When my father noticed the jujubes trips he was amused.

'They take the car out to go to the toilet,' he would say.

For me and for my father, this family which I had married into was an alien habitat. He meekly participated in all the social events, dinners and lunches, with good grace and a wry smile. He didn't stay long; his best friend, Nambiar's daughter was getting married, and he had to hurry back to give moral support.

Meanwhile I still had a long way to go towards becoming that wonderful Indian wife, which was meant to be my role, but my father's visit gave me a new perspective. He bolstered my self- worth – again.

Pakkiyam, the maid, ruled the kitchen and did not take kindly to my inept presence in her domain. On the one hand, I was Podi nona, little madam, and had to be treated with respect. On the other, what I knew about cooking could be safely put on a fingernail and forgotten. Worse still, I had never used piped gas for cooking and was lethal around it.

The kitchen itself was big, shabby and didn't have any wipe-clean surfaces; it looked dirty when it was not. I tried to make *Sambhar*, the catch-all dish cooked almost daily in India -- because any residual vegetables could be tossed into it, and if many visitors came at lunch time, it went far -- and produced something of the right colour and consistency but it tasted dull. It was served at lunch along with the *bonji* (French bean) curry and the *Thora malu* (Seer fish), which Pakkiyam produced daily.

Pakkiyam's vegetables were always served as curries in coconut milk sauce. Sri Lankan cooking was almost always coconut milk based. In India, coconut was ground to a paste most of the time, milk being used only in potato or meat stews. Coconut was also grated and used to garnish dry vegetable dishes. Pakkiyam cooked cabbage and beans in coconut milk day after day. I generally ate whatever was on the table, but didn't know how to make anything better.

My father had made a valiant, but belated effort to prepare me for being a wife. He sent me off to my maternal grandmother's house for two weeks, a few days before the wedding, with instructions to learn to cook a basic meal. It was a good week; my mother's two sisters, one two years younger than me and the other six months older, and I, spent the week gossiping. My grandmother kept admonishing me, asking me to be in the kitchen, but I ignored her. She didn't try very hard.

My husband's household operated within limited parameters meant for an invalid. My father-in-law ate the same breakfast daily, two fried eggs, two slices of bread and porridge; lunch and dinner were the concoction, which Pakkiyam cooked every day. My mother-in-law ate after her husband had eaten, and she had led him to the bathroom, washed him and put him to bed. She talked to him like an infant, repeating things loudly. Food for my husband and me was left covered on the table for whatever time Balan came home, twice a day.

Every evening, my father-in-law would get

dressed in his cream suit and bow tie for a drive to the beach. He was one of the first few Indians who had gone to the United Kingdom for education; I saw no other like him anywhere in Ceylon. He was tall and fair and could easily pass for an Englishman. Decades after coming back to India and then Ceylon, he comported himself according to his version of a British gentleman;

When these men went overseas, in the early part of the twentieth century, funeral rites would be performed for them -- they may never come back. His wife was left at home in Alathur for the seven years it took him to return. And when he did, he had to undergo ritual purification to be allowed into society. This was conducted in front of a huge, blazing fire, by holy men, and was supposed to signify rebirth after 'dying' when they returned from foreign lands. He had been doing a medical degree in Edinburgh; he brought back his daily routine of English breakfast with fried eggs and white bread, his porridge habit and his suit and tie.

A mile away from my home in Colombo, Kamala's husband had epicurean tastes. Whenever I went there I ate rich meat and fish curries, cooked in large quantities of butter and oil. Nadesan was a happy man, with a huge laugh, and lots of time for the people he liked. He took a liking to me and my father.

Nadesan had passed the highly competitive Ceylon Civil Service exams as a young man of twenty and worked his way up over the years to become Secretary to the UNP Prime Minister, Kotelawala. When Kotelawala was unseated in the fifties and S.W.R.D Bandaranaike of the Sri Lanka

Freedom Party became Prime Minister, Nadesan felt obliged to resign. So here was a man who had occupied an important government post, with now nothing to do but sit on the Boards of several companies. At one stage he was editor of the Times of Ceylon, and subsequently owned an antique store full of priceless Dutch and Chinese antiques. In between all these occupations, he grew roses and orchids and for some time, he was the President of the World Orchid Federation. Clearly a man looking for something fulfilling to do.

Still, I missed Naani's cooking, especially the love that was infused into all that she cooked. I missed the *Idlis* (rice and black-gram cakes) and *Doshas* with coconut *chutney*, which we ate for breakfast, and the many variations on vegetables. I missed the fried river-fish and the sweets she made from rice. And all this missing got more acute when I became pregnant. I wanted to go home.

28

Things became interesting in my Colombo home when my other sister-in-law, Leila, came home. She was married to an Indian army man and had no delusions of wealth or grandeur. She had a five-year old son with her, and a five-month old baby girl.

'Might as well get used to babies,' she said to me. She showed me how to pin a nappy on a baby, and recruited me into baby-sitting. Leila also took a good look at the food in the house and declared that she needed proper food.

'I need to feed my girl and I must eat, and drink lots of milk.' She marched into the kitchen and Pakkiyam gave way with bad grace. Leila cooked lentils and vegetables and ordered fish other than the pallid Seer fish, which was the fish in our household up to then.

'You are not going to live on Mama's silly food, *baba,* are you? You need proper food.' She addressed everybody in the house impartially as *baba.*

She bustled off in many directions and did wondrous things with the household.

'I need to talk to you,' she said to me one day when my mother-in-law was not around. 'Why are you living in this huge mausoleum with these old people?'

My father had instructed me to behave kindly and

not upset the old people. I didn't say that to Leila.

'Look,' she said. 'Kumaran and Vatsala live in their own home.'

This was true. Balan's younger brother and his wife lived ten minutes away in their own home.

'You should get out of here. Learn to run a home.'

This was not one of my ambitions, but I could see the advantages. Leila started getting regular newspapers and searching for a flat for me to move into. Eventually, I found an annex in the rarefied atmosphere of Cinnamon Gardens and moved out. Maybe, I thought, just maybe, Balan would get interested in his new life and stop acting like a bachelor.

Leila and I went shopping in Titus Store for pans and buckets, mops and mugs. She was thrifty unlike the rest of the family and I could recognise the directions she pointed out to me. She knew where to go for inexpensive linen and curtains. Balan was totally uninterested in any of this.

The expected realignment to family that I anticipated from Balan never happened. He went straight from work to his parent's home and came back to our flat after his drinking sessions with his friends. I had clearly lost out. It was much later, when we moved to a remote little town in Nigeria that Balan finally came home.

I went out looking for books and had limited success – books were too expensive. This was not an aspect of books I had considered in Thalassery. My father had a little revolving bookcase behind his bed and within reach; a changing collection appeared in that shelf every now and then as if by magic. In Colombo, I got magazines instead of books. The Life, Time and The Week were within my means and I took a bundle home the first time I went looking in Fort and in Pettah. I spent most of my afternoons in bed reading those magazines; I could get used to this, I thought.

With pregnancy, and not enjoying the Ceylonese food, or indeed my own cooking, which was lacklustre, I lost a great deal of weight, and literally counted the days to going home. Meanwhile I learned to cook rice and a few simple dishes by trial and error. Balan didn't mind what I put in front of him so long as it looked like food and smelled like food; perfect situation for me.

To a large extent I had been immured from the world outside in Bullers Road as well in Cinnamon Gardens.. The world, however crashed into all of us in the spring of 1958. The Sinhalese had mounted a merciless offensive on the Tamils in Ceylon and it was beginning to get closer every day.

S.W.R.D Bandaranaike, leader of the Sri Lanka Freedom Party and Prime Minister in 1958, passed legislation that announced that Sinhalese from then on would become the official language of Sri Lanka. This was the only language that would be used in government offices and civil services. The Tamil's saw this as a direct, unequivocal effort to exclude them from the Civil Services. Many had to resign their positions in Government posts because they were not fluent in Singhalese.

This was followed by more punitive legislation and exclusive politics, which eventually led to the

242

birth of the LTTE, the Liberation Tigers of Tamil Eelam, which demanded a separate Tamil state. A fierce and merciless civil war followed, culminating in the destruction of the LTTE in 2009.

In 1958, Tamils were getting beaten up and sometimes killed in the areas of Colombo and its outskirts, where the Sinhalese were in a majority. They were also being accosted, cars set on fire, and men assaulted in the centre of Colombo, and on the trains that came in from the north, which was Tamil territory. At this time, the Tamils had not yet organised themselves for defence or retaliation.

One evening, Balan came home agitated.

'Blue murder out there,' he said. 'Muni Aiyyah got beaten up, no men? In front of Walker Sons. Buggers are going mad.' Muni Aiyyah was a Tamil colleague.

'When Muni Aiyyah went to his car, which was parked in front and got into it, Sinhalese thugs rocked the car until it overturned, pulled him out and beat him up. Jainz just phoned me – I was working late,' Balan continued. Jainz was another colleague.

'How did you – ' I asked.

'I was lucky – my car was parked behind the office; I sneaked out through the back door.'

Balan was disturbed and angry.

'They are making them recite the *Jathakas*. I was born here, I speak fluent Sinhalese, but I don't know them. They say you are Tamil if you don't know the jathakas.'

'What are Jathakas? I asked.

'Only the Buddhists know the Jathakas -- chants about Buddha. They are stories of Buddha's previous incarnations and considered sacred incantations.

'In that case, don't go to the office until this settles,' I said.

Balan was not listening. He sounded scared and angry at the same time.

'They'll look at you and know that you are not Sinhalese,' he said to me. You can't speak the language anyway. And don't wear a *pottu* on your forehead. They think only Tamils wear *pottus*.'

During the riots, more than three hundred people were killed, most of them Tamils.

It is the custom in Kerala for women to go home for the first pregnancy in the seventh month. I was not concerned with the baby to come, or my husband, or anyone or anything else in Colombo; I wanted out.

I knew Balan would move back to his parents' home the day I left, and he did. When I returned to Ceylon many months later, I had to go back to live with his parents and start searching for another home. Meanwhile, Balan's ageing father had died while I was in India and his mother was planning to return to India to live in her old home.

29

I travelled back to India on a rainy July day. When the small Fokker friendship plane taking me home flew over the sea, I was busy vomiting into paper bags. It was just as well that there were only myself and the air-hostess in the cabin. There had been a full load until all of them, to the last man and woman got off in Jaffna, the short stop in the north of Ceylon.

The Fokker flew low over the sea and I could see the breakers down below. Until the land came into view. India! I cried, I had not fully realised how much I needed to get home. I was surprised at the strength of my emotion.

I knew my father would come to Trichy to meet me, but, when the plane landed and I reached the Customs hall, I was met by a large woman in a brown sari with a badge, which declared her a customs officer. I could see my suitcase had already been opened, and the contents spilled on to a desk; a man was going through them item by item.

'Come,' the Amazonian woman said. 'I sech.' She couldn't communicate much in English and I did not know enough Tamil. I was going on cryptic sounds.

She took me by my shoulders to a changing cubicle and pointed to my clothes, making a sign that I should take them off . She stood outside while I took my sari off, hung it on the wooden partition of the cubicle and stood there, befuddled. Why am I being searched? Whom to ask?

She peeked in and signalled for me to take my under-skirt off as well. This was getting serious. She could see I was very pregnant and weary with it. She pointed to my behind and signalled that she needed to search my rectum. I said, 'No.' I was close to tears. I pointed to my stomach and placed my hands over it – no one was going to put their fat official fingers inside me.

She went out again and talked to a man who had come by just then outside my cubicle. They talked loudly and hurriedly for a moment, then she came inside.

'Mishtek,' she said, not looking at my face. She took my clothes from where they were hanging and returned them to me. She went away, almost running. I draped my sari on again clumsily; the blue nylex kept slipping through my trembling fingers, so that took a while. I went to the carousel and collected my suitcase, which was going round and round alone. As I reached the exit, my discomfiture had turned to outrage.

Father was waiting at the exit with a friend of his working in Customs. Clearly, Achan had brought reinforcement, Indian style, to help me to come out without being harassed. The officer explained:

'We had information that someone was smuggling a large amount of precious stones, but there was no one but you on that plane. Looks like they got wind of us and got off at Jaffna.

'Our regional collector was here; I couldn't even show my face, let alone vouch for you.'

My father was so used to the waters parting for

him in Thalassery, he just couldn't fathom that there were situations in which his magic couldn't work.

We travelled back to Thalassery by train; he looked after me as though I was precious and fragile; How did I manage the last few months without this unconditional love?

When I returned home, I was back to where I had begun; I could safely leave Naani and Achan to look after me; I could cease to be vigilant. The baby was not due for another two months.

The morning after I arrived I had my first *Iddli* breakfast in a long while. I thought, it was just the lack of my usual Kerala food that had led to my unhappiness. Perhaps it was the pregnancy, which made me obsessive about food.

I had seen a doctor once in Colombo, after that I had not attended any ante-natal clinics in; I doubt the practice existed at that time. It was the same in India. I would have my baby the way women in that part of the world had babies, with the local midwife attending. Nobody did any blood tests or urine tests. My aunt instructed me not to sit for long periods. The baby's head will become flat and wide and it will become harder to deliver, she cautioned.

Indeed everything connected to birth, In Kerala, was the territory of the women, especially the old ones, and all that was associated with death was in the territory of men. The women were not allowed to accompany the body, even of a dead husband, on his final journey to the pyre.

I told my father what Velyamma had said about walking; he decided this was something he could help with. Every evening he marched me out for a

247

walk, large stomach preceding me. Men in Thalassery did not normally take pregnant women walking, even husbands. So this was another thing for our neighbours to fuss and gawp at.

Achan also called his doctor and insisted he looked after me. The doctor was a personal friend and sent a junior doctor to see me. She had been two years ahead of me in school and I knew her and her family well. She talked to me, asked about my sleep habits and what I ate and went away. The midwife came next. She was masterful – she did a urine test and told me I was fine. She was a little uncertain of the dates though.

My velyamma said my stomach was descending and she couldn't see me lasting out till August. All in all, it was a strangely unintrusive confinement. I got back to my old reading habits, starting with a book about the *Reorganisation of the States of India* by K M Panikkar. They were now organised on a linguistic basis with Kerala including all the Malayalam speaking areas. The princely states of Cochin and Travancore were now part of Kerala and the seat of government for all of it was in Thiruvananthapuram. Our umbilical connection with Madras was gone.

After a week in Thalassery I realised why pregnant women went home to have babies – they would be comprehensively cared for and cossetted. Coming from the houses of mother-in-laws, who were indifferent, they could now relax and enjoy being pregnant.

On the day before my son was born, Velyamma insisted it was full moon the next day, and I would give birth then. No one took any notice. When I woke up the next day, early in the morning, I was already experiencing contractions, which became stronger and more painful as the afternoon came.

As usual visitors came and went, but I was not allowed to mention the status quo to anyone. I had to bite down on my lips and wait for the visitors to go. Having a baby was a personal and family matter; you didn't want outsiders in on it.

Just as my Velyamma had said, my son was born on full-moon day; he was premature by three weeks and small by western standards but par for Indian babies. I remember the doctor had no role in this event; the midwife was experienced and confident. She came to the house daily for a fortnight after and taught me to breastfeed and care for my baby. The doctor came once – it was a friendly visit rather than a professional one. She brought me a copy of Benjamin Spock's book on baby care.

My father was nonplussed, didn't know what to say or do. What was his role in all this? He would put his head round the door of my room once every day to ask me whether I was comfortable.

'You can give the baby a bottle,' he kept saying. He didn't want his daughter to have any problems, but I insisted on breastfeeding. One day he brought down that old bottle from his chest of drawers, which had been my bottle when I was born. I was touched.

He also sent the doctor around to discuss family planning with me. The doctor was uncomfortable.

'Your father says you need to think of family planning. Babies one after the other will ruin your health.' Achan was still trying to safeguard my health. 'That man is crazy – he's always worrying about you.'

'I will discuss it with my husband,' I said.

I didn't see my husband for a very long five months. The baby started turning over on to his stomach after three months, and recognising people. The household revolved around his routines.

According to custom, women from the husband's family are supposed to pay a ceremonial visit soon after the birth of the baby. This is their affirmation that this baby belongs to their family and they are acknowledging that. They normally bring clothes and sometimes a gold waist-chain for the baby. They also bring money to cover the expenses of the confinement; in my case, none of this happened.

Once in two or three weeks I'd get a letter from my husband. I couldn't respond as I was not allowed to read or write for forty days; the idea was that this would harm my eyes seriously. He knew this was the case, but it still annoyed him. I was frustrated at not being allowed my books; I was even more annoyed my husband and his family showed no interest in my son.

Soon the neighbours started asking pointed questions about when my in-laws would come, did they send money for the child... How much? My father ignored the lot, bought a gold chain for my son and seemed happy to have us at home. When he was free he would ask that the baby be left near him on a mat on the veranda and they communicated with each other in their different ways.

When Kitta was three months old my father-in-law died and his family came to Dhanushkodi on the southern tip of India to immerse his ashes in the sea. Balan accompanied them but did not bother to travel the few hours north to see his new son.

I was disgusted and wondered whether I should return to Ceylon at all. Balan eventually turned up when Kitta was over five months old and I travelled back to Colombo with him. I never found out what made Balan do or not do anything. He was now in his mother's house, quite content to revert to being the faithful son, but I insisted on finding a home and moving out. If there was a soft spot there, I never found it. Yet, I knew nothing he did was premeditated; he just let the days pass taking the line of least resistance, the same easy path he took when he consented to get married, though he would have been just as happy remaining a bachelor

In Thalassery, my family had never used napkins for babies. He was cleaned. and washed with warm water. I learned how to fold a napkin and pin it on from Spock. I learned how to burp him and hold him. I had a great deal to learn about babies; Balan of course was not remotely interested.

My husband's family had the right to name the first baby and they decided to call him Radhakrishnan, after the Indian President, Sarvepalli Radhakrishnan. A long name for a small person. My father called him Kitta for short and that stuck. All Krishnans become Kittans in Kerala like Richards become Dicks. Today, in the university where he teaches, he is called Kit.

My family continued to pamper me -- now the objective was to return me in pristine, pre-pregnancy condition to my husband. Every morning, an outside woman, Yeshoda, came to our house. She would put a large copper pot on the three-stone fire in the bathroom. While the water heated up she would put medicinal oils on me, and massage my stomach muscles. Then the hot water, as hot as I could stand, would be slapped on to my stomach.

My diet was rich: mutton soups, vegetables, fish and lots of milk. In addition the vaidyan had prescribed some *lehyams*, thick, slightly gritty gels that were supposed to purify blood and make me fat. Looking big was important, because the husband and his family would expect a fatted calf back.

A woman came on a regular basis to remove the stained cloths used in the delivery and after, and wash them and return them to me. She belonged to a special caste called *vannaathi* and it was her traditional job.

I once asked her where she washed the cloths. She told me she collected the material from many houses where babies had been born and washed them in a small pond. I knew where the pond was – it was filthy. When I told her that she could not do my washing, she was outraged; it was hers by right. So my father paid her as if she had completed the forty days of washing, which she would have normally done, and she went away angry. She cursed loudly. I made arrangement for my cloths to be washed and disinfected at home.

The restrictions attached to childbirth were beginning to annoy me as I did not believe in any of the reasons for the various taboos. I was not allowed to walk outside in the compound after dusk because an evil goddess, called *Ottamulachi*, (the single-breasted woman) would harm me; my breast milk would dry up. I was confined to my bedroom for twenty-eight days and to the house for forty. I began wondering whether having the baby in India had been a good idea after all. I enjoyed the unconditional love and coddling but did not trust the slapdash hygiene for me and the baby.

The naming ceremony took place, as usual, on the twenty-eighth day; this was another occasion where the role of the father's family was central, but nobody turned up. Again, the neighbours twittered, asked questions and some said I had been divorced by my husband. It felt like that sometimes.

30

Marriages are taken to be forever in India, as in 'death do us part' literally – there is no questioning its efficacy -- It was always the union of two families and you treated it with respect. If the man did not beat up his wife, chase other women, get drunk on a regular basis or deny the wife housekeeping money, he was considered a good husband. Even if he did all these things, wives were supposed to 'put up and shut up.'

When I returned to Colombo, I was far from unhappy. I had my son and he took up most of my time. Leila was good company meanwhile, and after a few months, I had a new home to organise. I was beginning to break all the self-made rules of my husband's family. Instead of finding a home in central Colombo far beyond my means and getting into debt, I decided to go into the suburbs and pay a quarter of the rent.

'*Not a single Nair stays outside Colombo,*' my mother-in-law informed me angrily. Was she concerned that Balan would not be within call? She need not have worried. I ignored her and moved to Wattala, about six miles from Colombo. It was a cluster of homes which were occupied by middle income families like us. There were five houses in that compound and for the first time, I made friends with women like me. Balan continued to go straight

254

from work to his mother's house and then for drinks to his club; he came home around nine in the evening.

On weekends a friend of his would come down to stay with us. He was a good man and I think, felt guilty about spending every weekend with us. The two men, Balan and Jayaratnam, went out together Saturdays and Sundays, and came back late in the evening. This was a pre-marriage habit and they carried on with it. I had no role in any of this. Balan continued with his faux bachelor existence.

Nearest to us in the compound lived Chitty, a colleague of Balan's also with a first baby of Kitta's age. Every evening, around six, I would hear his car driving into the gravel front of his house and braking. I would wonder why Balan did not want to come home – I would tell myself that I was never good wife material and this just confirmed it. As an only child, I was used to making my own entertainments; I got back to reading, took long walks in the neighbourhood.

Sometimes, I would ask Balan to send the car and driver for me to do the shopping in town. The driver would turn up around two in the afternoon and I would drive into Pettah and buy what I needed for the house. It would be close to five-thirty when I finished; I would ask the driver to pass by Balan's office and pick him up. The driver would run up with my message that I was waiting in the car downstairs. Balan invariably told the driver to take me home and return the car. After the third or fourth time this happened, I could see the pity on the driver's face and stopped asking him to go by at Balan's office.

The four other families living in the compound were young couples like us and friendly. We helped each other with lifts into town, and in the evenings, we congregated for a gossip session in the common area. I grew Cannas in front of my little house, dressed the front window with cheap blue calico and acquired an *Amme* (ayah) called Jane to cook for me. In the evenings she took my baby for walks; baby and Jane adored each other.

From Jane, Kitta learned his first few words of Sinhalese by the age of one. I knew little Sinhalese but learned enough to talk to Jane. My second baby, Raghu, was born seventeen months later; I wanted a large family to make up for lack of siblings and absconding husband and I was succeeding. I was back into my books and becoming more self-sufficient by the day.

Balan's family never came visiting once, even when my second son was born. I wondered whether they were annoyed I had moved to the suburbs. Six miles was too far out of Colombo for them. My sisters in law, the Malayalee women who were married to Balan's brothers, turned up with gifts for my son – they knew the Kerala protocol.

However, just when I thought I was nicely settled in Wattala, and life seemed almost stable, our landlord announced all five of us tenants would have to move. He had built himself a mansion in the compound next to ours, and he wanted more elbow room. We found out about the level of his ambitions in that direction, the day of his house-warming party, to which all the tenants next door were invited.

The party went on for three days; so did the music

and loud laughter. I could hear the incessant sounds of raucous conviviality next door. My husband dropped in on the party on the second day and came back after several hours, floored by the free-flowing liquor as well as the scale of the celebration. He fell into bed and did not get up till the next afternoon.

When he became reasonably compos mentis he told me about the party next door. Liquor, he said, not only flowed inside the house, there were guests quietly walking out with bottles of champagne hidden under their kurtas (long shirts). No one knew Balan and no one greeted him or talked to him. If the man had a wife, she was nowhere in evidence. Our landlord was famous in Ceylon for having built his wealth on the sale of dry fish, and on this day he was proclaiming the extent of that franchise.

He had *'imported'* hostesses from overseas and they cavorted on a stage in the back garden. Several ministers of the government were in evidence enjoying the lavish hospital and building up an obligation for the future. All of this was out of Balan's comfort zone, and he came back fairly quickly.

We started looking for another home and ended up in *Battaramulla*, on the other side of town, even further away from Colombo. This area was a Sinhalese stronghold and there was some anxiety because we were clearly not Sinhalese. There was one Indian couple there, however, and we moved. I knew nothing about these areas, or indeed, who lived where in Colombo. I excused myself saying I was busy raising two infants within seventeen months of each other and had no time to find out who dominated in *Wellawatta* or *Mount Lavinia.*

257

I blamed myself: why did I not make more of an effort to melt into the scene, enjoy it? Many years later I spent large tracts of time living in Nigeria, Sierra Leone, Uganda, Zambia and Malawi and I was part of the landscape. My colleagues and neighbours dropped by casually and I would also walk into their verandas for a gossip session when I had finished walking my dogs. I knew everything that happened in the lives of my friends and they knew about my family: who had passed what exams, what grades they got, which University they were applying for...

I didn't like the steamed *Matoke* Ugandans ate for their meals, but I would eat a little to get a taste for it. I didn't succeed. Instead I learned to make groundnut stew and *Plassas* – potato or cassava leaves, cooked and pounded into a rich sauce with oils and flavourings -- delicious. I knew which tribe lived in which part of the country and their local rituals. Yet, in Ceylon, I was the outsider.

I made one friend in Battaramulla – Mrs Senivaratne lived across from us and I went for my walks with her and my babies. Meanwhile, at home, I had company in my house, again. My lovely sister-in-law, Leila returned to India when her husband came back from a peacekeeping mission in East Asia. My brother-in-law lost his job, his wife went back to India and he and his mother came to live with us.

Balan came home earlier from work, I let my mother-in-law take over the kitchen, which she loved, and we spent some months together. We got to know each other better, and if not exactly friends, we lived as an extended family without conflict. She and her son returned to India eventually and Balan got transferred north to Jaffna.

Balan had spent his entire childhood in Colombo, gone to school there and worked there. Colombo people are a special breed like the Mumbaikars of India. They are not happy anywhere else. Balan felt life had somehow demoted him. If he was working in Colombo I doubt he would have considered migrating to Nigeria. But Jaffna was easy to discard.

In Jaffna, rents were low; the problem was to find a reasonably equipped house, with wipe-clean surfaces, running water, indoor toilet... Colombo had spoiled me for any compromise with hygiene -- I had two infants to care for.

There was not much choice; Balan was a weekend husband for several weeks, staying at the government guest house while he looked for a suitable house. What he found eventually was short of what I wanted – the house had an outside toilet and a long drop toilet inside, not one that flushed. So we were back to the shit cart and the daily removals.

Otherwise it was a nice house with large windows and plenty of light. I had two neighbours near who lived in identical houses and that seemed promising. Both had children slightly older than mine but were friendly and helpful. One spoke only Tamil and the other was a burgher family, who spoke English and Sinhalese. The Sinhalese *Amme*, Jane, did not accompany us to distant Jaffna, known to be the stronghold of the Tamils, so now I had to do the cooking, cleaning, looking after the children, and the laundry.

Balan conjured up a Hoover washing machine, a

top-loader, and a floor polisher from his firm; that helped, but I barely managed the housework from day to day. Now Balan recruited Ronald, a young man from the building site that he managed, to cook for us. Life became a little easier, but the Jaffna sand got into my skin and I broke out in eczemas on my toes and elbows. Did it get into my soul as well and destroy my self-confidence?

My father came visiting; when he saw how I was running from one chore to another, he was concerned.

'Why don't you come home for a little while, take some time off from all this?'

Home. Where was home really? Where my boys were and the people around cared. I went to India briefly when my second son, Raghu, was ten months old, and I conspired to get out of Jaffna, maybe even Ceylon.

Nigeria had just become independent in 1960. Three of Balan's contemporaries at Technical College went to Ghana and Nigeria. When they came back on furlough they visited and spoke highly of the places where they were working; they were beaming with the assurance of hard currency accumulated in their bank accounts. They encouraged him to apply for posts in Nigeria and Ghana.

The Crown agents came around recruiting teachers and engineers again in 1961. They got as far as Madras, but the Ceylon government refused them permission to recruit from Ceylon. The government impounded the passports of some doctors and engineers who were planning to leave. But they were half-hearted with that.

I persuaded Balan to apply; he went to Madras to be interviewed; it was only an hour by plane from Jaffna to Madras. He was offered a post in Nigeria, but he was suddenly scared. He did not resign his job at Walkers for many months after, and kept Nigeria dangling while he made up his mind. The prospect of living anywhere except Ceylon was hard for Balan to contemplate. Eventually he decided to go.

I was elated; I had come to the end of my reluctant truce with Ceylon; I was ready for other places.

In March of 1962, we left Ceylon; after that I went back two or three times for holidays. In those four years in Ceylon, I gained huge self-awareness, most of it not complimentary to myself. I realised I had a grade E marriage, which I could not nurture as long as I lived in Ceylon. Would Nigeria be any better? Couldn't be worse. But, before Nigeria, there were a few issues to consider.

When Balan told his mother that we were going to Nigeria soon, she was, predictably, not happy. I was excited to think of that whole new world opening out in front of me, but I had not considered how it would affect our families. My mother-in-law had three other children resident in Colombo and she still felt anxious; how was Achan going to react when he heard that his precious daughter was going half a world away? I asked myself.

I went to Thalassery with my boys, in February of 1962, a month before Balan and I were scheduled to depart for Nigeria. Plenty of time to reassure my father, perhaps myself too. My father watched quietly as I went about my preparations for the journey. I shopped for a list of things that friends of Balan already in Nigeria said we should stock up on, as they would be impossible to get in Eastern Nigeria. Top of the list was saris to take with me; there were no sari shops in Eastern Nigeria. I bought kohl and pottu to last eighteen months, which was as long as I would be away, and got my tailor to make under-skirts for me and shorts and shirts for my sons, now four and two years old. I also collected spices for curry and my maid in India roasted them and made curry powder for me.

The quality time I had planned to spend with Achan, however, shrank rapidly, frittered away talking to friends and family who came by to say good-bye and give me addresses of other Indians in Africa – never mind that they were in East Africa, most of them. Africa, to many of my acquaintances in Thalassery at that time, was just one huge, dark, unknown place.

Achan put up with the stream of visitors who came to see me off, ordering cups of tea from the kitchen and dodging questions about how he felt. Till, one evening, he came home from work and there were no visitors. I was out shopping and came in late; he was sitting alone in the dark on the veranda as I dragged myself up the steps wearily, loaded with my loot.

'What are you buying these days so frantically?' he asked, as I staggered in and threw my plastic bags on a chair. There was a slight, familiar edge to the question. A smile waiting to break through.

'Can't get stuff in Enugu, saris and such like.'

'It is true the women in Africa didn't wear much in the past.' Achan was speaking slowly, question marks all over his face. 'But that was decades ago. I understand they wear clothes now-a-days, don't they? Quite colourful too.' He was enjoying this now. 'Can't you wear the clothes they wear, instead of carting India along with you?

After that I stopped my shopping trips.

Achan continued in the role of benign on-looker as I collected addresses of Indians in Uganda and Kenya and Tanzania, all of whom I should 'look up' when I got to Nigeria!

'Mmm,' he said one day when another posse' of visitors had come and gone. 'Lots of trips to visit strangers the other side of Africa, eh?'

'And,' he added, 'If you want to see Indians, you should stay here; there are six hundred and thirty million of us here.'

Glossary

The names by which relatives are addressed and respect is shown to elders:

Achan   Father

Amma   Mother

Ettan   Elder brother. So Appu would be
addressed as Appuettan.

Echi/ edathy   Elder sister. So Naani becomes
Naaniedathy.

Ammamma   Mother's mother

Velyamma   Grandmother or elderly aunt

Velyachan   Grandfather or elderly uncle

Ammaman   Uncle